THE BOSS IS IN

THE BOSS IS IN:

incapable, incompetent, ineffective,
inferior, inflated- egotist, ingrate,
inhuman, insane, insecure, insensitive,
insincere, insufferable, insulting,
intolerable, ...

ROBERT M. HARDY

Order this book online at www.trafford.com
or email orders@trafford.com

Most Trafford titles are also available at major online book retailers.

Names have been changed for the key players in the cases to protect the privacy of the participants

Cover illustration by Alisha Koepf

Note for Librarians: A cataloguing record for this book is available from Library
and Archives Canada at www.collectionscanada.ca/amicus/index-e.html

Printed in Victoria, BC, Canada.

ISBN: 978-1-4269-0380-9 (Soft)

*Our mission is to efficiently provide the world's finest, most comprehensive
book publishing service, enabling every author to experience success.
To find out how to publish your book, your way, and have it available
worldwide, visit us online at www.trafford.com*

Trafford rev. 01/20/2010

 www.trafford.com

North America & international
toll-free: 1 888 232 4444 (USA & Canada)
phone: 250 383 6864 ✦ fax: 812 355 4082

For Laurie

Publication of this book has been delayed. I had given myself a deadline to finish the draft, and take a vacation for a few days in Tucson, Arizona. On that same day, my youngest daughter, Laurie Linn Hardy (1962-2008), passed away unexpectedly in Sarasota, Florida. Laurie was looking forward to doing my proofreading. It took me a while to decide to finish it.

Laurie was very supportive and excited about the book. I would not now want to disappoint her. I hope that it would meet with her satisfaction and approval. I hope it meets with yours.

Foreword

By William J. Premerlani, Ph.D.

The first time that I met Bob Hardy was on a job interview with the company we both wound up working for, far longer than either of us ever imagined that we would. The hiring manager, the man that Bob worked for, forgot that I was coming in that day and was out of town on a business trip. Bob was embarrassed for him. I should have taken the oversight as a forewarning of things to come and run away as fast as I could, but I did not. Bob's warmth and humanity overcame my better judgment.

Bob was busy that day with other things, including an important presentation, but somehow he found time to interview me. Together, we decided that the position was right for me, and that we would enjoy working together. I took the position. More that 30 years later, I can honestly say that I have no regrets. I was fortunate to know Bob, and to have him for a lifelong friend. He made everything we did together more interesting, and helped me weather the stormy seas of corporate America. Over time we invented some things, worked on interesting and challenging problems, and made money for our employer. We had some good laughs.

We also witnessed some events we could hardly believe, many strange and astounding things. Even today, I have trouble imagining that some of the things I recall actually happened. Bob helps me know that I didn't dream it. These things really happened. Many of them involved me and I witnessed nearly all of the rest. These are true events that Bob and I picked apart and analyzed like bridge hands that had played out wrong, to see how they might have played differently. Sometimes we were angry at the injustice, incompetence and insensitivity that we saw. Sometimes we laughed. Sometimes we cried. On one occasion when management incompetence contributed to the death of an employee, we thought for sure there would be a lawsuit that never materialized.

What you have in your hands is a collection of true stories of management blunders, stories that Bob and I lived. We hope that you find them interesting and entertaining, and learn something from them. Then you will not do these sorts of things to others, and you can better defend yourself if you find yourself in a similar situation.

- **Bill Premerlani**

Acknowledgements

I will start by thanking my long time buddy, Dr. Bill Premerlani. Without Bill's suggestion I might never have started this book. Without his encouragement, I might not have finished. Further, he reviewed all of the cases and helped me remember the facts of many and report them accurately.

Dr. Mike Blaha set the format for the cases in the book that we started to write, but didn't. The book was to be about business and engineering failures. Perhaps we will write a book together sometime. Thanks to Mike.

Thanks to Alisha Koepf who did the illustration for the cover. I discussed concepts for the cover with a local artist/arts teacher who turned the project over to her former art student, Alisha, who is my grand daughter. It wasn't easy to sketch a boss representing many of the bad "*in*" traits covered in the book.

Thanks go to my wife, Pat, for allowing me to spend many hours at my computer instead of being more sociable. Thanks also for making me take breaks away from the keyboard for health reasons. Then, she has been my chief proofreader.

Finally, I couldn't have written this book without all of the "*in*" managers I had the opportunity to observe. For this writing I have taken on the role of reporter. If things improve in the job relationships between employees and bosses as a result of this reporting, it will have provided some value. Based on the observations made collecting these stories, it is doubtful that any of our so-called "*in*" bosses will ever improve their management skills. At least, none of our samples ever did. However both the employees and the "*in*" bosses' bosses may become more aware in the art of detecting and dealing with the "*in*" boss situations. Typically they are not intentionally acting inappropriately, though some may be, as will be seen. Many are simply unaware that they are acting inappropriately. It is a tragedy all the way around when anyone thinks he/she is doing a good job when in fact he/she isn't. In fairness, some of the "*in*" bosses such as described are *in need* of medical attention, for which they may or may not be aware. Being aware, though, is not the same as taking corrective action.

Contents

Foreword   By William J. Premerlani, Ph.D.   vii

Acknowledgements   ix

About this Book   xiii
     Introduction   xiii
     The Boss Is In   xv
     Real Cases   xv
     Exit Strategy   xvi
     What Should the Employee do?   xvii
     The Employee-Boss   xviii
     Benefit   xix

There really are Good Bosses – In Memory of Oliver Dale Wertz,
     The Best Boss I ever had   xxiii

CASES

Case 1   EGOMANIA: The Over Egotistical Boss   1

Case 2   GLASS CEILING: Discrimination and Under the Table
     Hiring   5

Case 3   PLEASE LET GO: The Boss Who Wouldn't Delegate   11

Case 4   SEE NO EVIL: The Boss who looked the other way   16

Case 5   SHADE of GRAY: The Case of the Boss' Kickback   20

Case 6   DID WHAT? The No Results Boss   25

Case 7   WHISTLE BLOWER: The Boss Who Got Caught   29

Case 8   WINNER TAKE ALL: The Bosses' Power Struggle   33

Case 9   AFFAIRS of the OFFICE: The Boss' Trouble Maker   39

Case 10   CULTURE SHOCK: East is East, West is West   44

Case 11   MISS CONFIDENTIALITY: The (Non) Confidential
     Survey   50

Case 12   WHO'S THE BOSS: The Two Boss Dilemma   56

Case 13   AGE DISCRIMINATION: The Case Couldn't Lose   61

Case 14   HE'S UP, HE'S DOWN, HE'S UNWOUND: The
     Bi-Polar Boss   78

Case 15 STOLEN CREDIT: The Technology Thief   84

Case 16 ALPHA DOG: The Micro Manager Boss   89

Case 17 POLITICALLY CORRECT: But -- Deadly Gender
         Discrimination   95

Case 18 SODOMIZER: The Manager's Nickname   102

Case 19 ATTENTION PLEASE: The ADD/ADHD Boss   107

Case 20 WAKE UP: The Power Napper   114

Case 21 RELIGION FIRST: The Religious Boss   120

Case 22 UNLIKEABLE YOU: The Boss Just Doesn't Like You
         125

Case 23 WHAT'S UP, DOC? The Clueless Boss   130

About the Author   135

About this Book

Introduction

When I started writing this book it had a different name and covered different subject matter. I started with a group of my former colleagues to write a book of case studies about failures. Together, collectively, we had many years of experience in project engineering covering the gamut from aerospace lunar landings to microcircuits to financial systems. These projects all had two things in common. One -- they had never been done before, so there were no models for guides except for the experiences, training and imagination of the participants. They were in the interest of advancing the state of the art in the subject matter. Second -- all projects start, run and end. The ending may bring the satisfaction of success, or the disillusionment of failure. Regardless, it is the end, and the participants must go on to other projects.

We may learn as much, or more, from failures as we do from successes. We wanted our book to capture the wisdom that we gained from failures over the years. In writing my share of the cases for the book on failures, I noticed a common cause for project failures. Many would classify the most common failures as resulting from inappropriate management. Nothing failed for technical reasons. Management failures can be classified in numerous terms, including inadequate planning, under funding, personnel problems, wrong decisions and others. Sometimes good managers make wrong decisions. Timing is important, as the market may not be ready or we have missed the marketing window. On the other hand, the manager may be just plain bad. This should not be a surprise, as most of us, at one time or another, has had to deal with a bad boss.

I had a boss once who liked to tell the story of the manager who was given a toast on his leaving the company. The presenter said that Joe's project had been cancelled, through no fault of his own, and he was leaving the company. He then went back into Joe's employment history and told that Joe had left his previous company because of a project that failed, though through no fault of his own. Prior to that, Joe had left his employer because of a project that failed, again, "through no fault of his own". The speaker decided to stop at that point.

This is a book of stories of standalone cases. The cases cover a variety of characteristics exhibited by erratic behavior of individual bosses. They range from very simple to quite complicated. They each actually happened in a big company environment. Each case focuses on a snapshot or a moving account of happenings in a space of time. A case might even represent one day, or a few days or many months, in the life of a bad boss that exemplifies his/her typical behavior. The significant players are identified with fictitious names. The facts are given and then the case is analyzed. The outcomes are shown as the case actually played itself out in the longer term. See if you would come to the same conclusions, given the same facts. See if you agree with the actions taken, if any, by the company. See what you would do if faced with any one of the bosses caught in the acts described by these accounts.

So often the management governing over the bad manager turns deaf ears to employee complaints. How well a manager gets along with his/her employees is seldom a reason for a management change. The end result of the manager's job is the only important factor, as symptoms along the way go unnoticed. It is also an embarrassment to the management who hired a bad boss in the first place. They may also be less than perfect. They take notice, however, when they are made to look bad. The higher management has ways of getting rid of bad bosses in discrete ways. Some are not so different from the highly publicized golden parachutes given to exiting executives. It usually involves some compensation and assistance in moving to another job or to another company.

The factual events are presented, and the decisions and the outcomes are detailed. The reader may someday find him/herself in the same situation. On the other side, a reader may recognize him/herself in the boss' role and decide to change. If that happens, then this book will have served well.

The Boss Is In

I named this book, **THE BOSS IS IN: "in" as in (alphabetic order), incapable, incompetent, ineffective, inferior, inflated-egotist, ingrate, inhuman, insane, insecure, insensitive, insincere, insufferable, insulting, intolerable, ...** These are only a few of the many **"in"** words that may be used to describe bad bosses. Many are overlapping in scope. Labels alone do not adequately describe a bad boss, whereas descriptions of actions are more conclusive. Some bosses exhibit one or many of these symptoms.

Employees should always ask the question, "Is it the boss, or is it me?" And should the "in" word, "incompatible", apply? The employees may carry a boss who is "incompetent", in the simple sense of the word. Here, however, we look at the serious cases, cheating, lying, discriminating, stealing, cultural diversity and gender related problems. One has only to watch the news to be aware that these things go on in business, and in government. The higher the level of management, the more severe is the damage.

Some activity is in the reverse order of what one is accustomed to reading. There is also coverage of activity brought about by medical conditions. There are cases that might have simple solutions except for the reluctance of those involved to discuss taboos or politically incorrect issues.

Real Cases

In this book all cases of bad bosses are real. None are contrived. All have taken place to the knowledge of this writer. Many books teach the theories of good management. Many books expose the reader to varieties of dysfunctional bosses across many types of jobs. This book concentrates on bad managers in a big Fortune 500 type company, involving well-educated professional people. The focus is on bosses and employees, most of whom are career people in the company, or at least the employee is a career worker. Can the boss be rehabilitated? That might be the ideal case, but it rarely happens. Though a compromise might be worked out between the employee and the boss, thus allowing the work to go on.

None of this means that the cases presented here could not apply to a dollar store clerk (there is no dime store anymore) or a burger flipper. However, in these latter cases, the employee's most likely option would be to quit. That is particularly true if the boss is also the owner of the company.

It is important to look at the environment in which a bad boss is allowed to grow. Bad bosses come in many varieties and their effects may range anywhere from minor nuisances to loss of employment to life threatening tactics, and even leading to death. Did I say death? Yes, I have included a case where an employee died as the likely result of mismanagement. It could happen again at some other place and some other time!

Exit Strategy

Very few enter into a new job with an exit strategy in mind. This may vary, however, for someone with great expectations for moving upward in the company's management chain. In this book some of the cases involve the moving of an employee into a new organization and with a new boss, Others involve the new boss taking charge of an existing organization. It may be the boss' first managerial assignment.

It usually doesn't take long for an employee to determine that he/she has a bad boss. An employee should not allow himself to become a bad boss' victim. Upon recognition of a bad boss problem, the employee should start planning some way out of the bad situation. We've all heard the stories of marriages where one of the partners knows the other has certain "fixable" deficiencies. The "fixes" seldom work. General advice in business is: Don't waste your time. Move on. For the cases presented in this book, not a single manager improved or even changed his/her bad management style.

There is one bad situation that occurs when a boss discriminates based on age. The employee finds him/herself backed into a corner with no place to go. It is more likely that he will go to a job that requires the employee to hit the ground running rather than to offer long term potential. The long term potential is simply not there for the older employee. Such a case with few options is presented in this book.

Leaving the company after many years of vested interest is simply not an option, unless everything else fails. Fortunately, in a big company, transfers may be a solution, allowing the employee to remain with the company, thereby retaining full benefits earned over the duration. Transfers within a company may offer solutions for many bad employee-boss relationships. Transfers may also create bad relationships. There may be business cultural differences from one company component to another causing bad relationships, just as one might experience when moving to a different company. It generally is not the company that is bad, but the individual boss. This point may be argued, as some cases present the management style passed from the CEO on down to the lowest level of management. Many long-term employees believe that middle managers really run the company, as top managers come and go with little or no impact on the lower level employees. While that may be true in many instances, top management can set the business culture for the entire company.

What Should the Employee do?

When an employee is faced with a difficult or impossible boss, decisions have to be made. Can the employee live with the problem? If not, can the employee solve the problem, or does he/she need inside or outside help? The employee may have misconceptions about the role of Human Resources (HR). They refer to HR as "Human Relations". One should be aware that HR works for the company, and may very well try to solve problems, but is not the protector of the employee. The employer may have outsourced Employee Assistance Programs (EAP) that may or may not work.

Sometimes the boss' actions may be clearly illegal. The legal or justice system may not be a safe haven. As there are bad bosses, there are also bad judges. As there are crooked bosses, there are crooked lawyers and crooked judges. This will be shown in an important "bad boss" case. The cards are cut to the advantage of the company. After all, that's where the money is. A last resort situation may result in a lawsuit. A case presented here will show just how nasty a lawsuit can be.

The Employee-Boss

A dissatisfied employee may have more options depending on his/her level within the organization or company. We should not think of these bad bosses presented here as managing people only at the lowest level. The employee may be a boss him/herself. For an employee-boss the solution may be the toughest. This is the case where the upwardly mobile person may be facing a dead end because of a bad boss.

Almost everyone at any and all levels has a boss. Even the CEO has to satisfy the board of directors and ultimately the owners, or stockholders. The boss' boss may be a great boss, an average boss, or a lousy boss. The boss may be a strong boss or a weak boss. The boss may meet or exceed all of his/her management objectives without regard to how you, the employee, may perceive him/her. Management 101 teaches that one should never criticize the person in question, but rather the work or performance of the person. In talking about bad bosses, it becomes cloudy as to the distinction between one's performance and his/her personal character.

When I started my career in engineering, I additionally had earned a degree in Industrial Management. After a few years in engineering I received a promotion to the ranks of management. I thought that everyone wanted to advance within the ranks. On my first job as a boss I was giving a performance appraisal for one of my employees and gave a negative critique of the technician's report writing. I asked him how he expected to get promoted unless he improved his writing skills. He informed me that he didn't want to be promoted, that he was satisfied in his job, and that reporting was my job, not his. Report writing was not in his job description. I didn't have to think very long to concede that he was doing a fine job in his specialty, and that I would take care of the reports. We had a very good relationship for the several years he worked for me.

I had learned that many excellent performers were satisfied to remain as excellent performers on their current jobs. They should be rewarded accordingly. Promotion into a higher-level job may not at all suit the employee. Recognition and money come to mind as a better option. After having gone through a few years of confusion, I have since found that my own passion was really in engineering. I have worked with many engineers and scientists who have reached very enviable heights in their fields through discovery and invention.

There are classifications of managers that may be applied when promoting a person into a management position or upgrading to a higher level of management. There is the 1) *authoritarian*, that is, he/she bosses by order of given authority. Such is the case with the military. Next, there is the authority by 2) *expertise*. The person most expert in the work of the group is in charge. Sometimes this goes well, and sometimes not. A person may be a technical expert, but a lousy manager. Third, there is 3) *deference to age*, and perhaps experience. Deference to age is natural to our culture. Fourth, there is the 4) *democratic* selection of the manager. After the selection, the democratic process may or may not work. Finally, there is the one with the 5) *natural leadership* capability.

This book simply looks at bosses and how they treat employees, written from the perspective of the employee, with a management analysis. See if you agree with the analyses and the way in which some of the problems were handled.

Benefit

It's possible, but not probable, that a person can go through a complete career without ever having a bad boss. A concept is championed by Jack Welch, former CEO of General Electric Company, and Suzy Welch in the book, *Winning,* 2005. It is a theory called the 20-70-10 rule that might predict that twenty percent would exhibit outstanding characteristics, seventy percent good or average, and that ten percent would be so bad that they should be fired.

In 1968, Laurence J. Peter wrote the classic, *The Peter Principle: Why things always go wrong.* "In a hierarchy every employee tends to rise to his level of incompetence." Such is based on the principle that employees who excel in their jobs are promoted up to the job at which they can no longer meet the requirements of the job. A recognized solution is that an employee should be observed to be working at a position above his/her current level before promotion.

My observation has been that employees are the happiest working for a long time boss, as opposed to working for a newly appointed boss. It stands to reason that a long term boss would be good at his/her job, having performed it over and over again until he/she got it right. Such a boss may not be good for everyone, though. A non-promotable boss may stand in the way of a promotable employee. There also may be employees who want to take risks, that may not be compatible with the style of a long time boss. Avoiding risks may be how he/she got to be a long time boss.

Some employees need and want to be bossed. Others do not. I heard the owner of an automobile repair shop say that he didn't want employees whose hands he needed to hold on the job. Likewise, most employees don't want that either. I heard a senior vice president of General Electric Company, the director of Corporate Research and Development, say that "managing researchers is like herding cats – impossible". I have worked in Eastern Europe following the collapse of the USSR and seen very highly educated people begging for bosses. They didn't want people thinking for them, what they really wanted was permission to act. I detected that attitude to result from the culture inherited from the previous authoritarian government. In visits to Asia I have detected employees wanting to conform and blend into the activities of the group. Managers and employees in these cultures tend to act accordingly. When an employee changes companies, he/she may be shocked by a difference in the business cultures from one company to another.

These cases presented here are all different. They show bosses with different characteristics that cause them to be considered bad bosses. A boss may be bad in relationships with only one employee, a select group of employees or all employees. Also a really bad boss may exhibit numerous bad characteristics. Are there some threads that might tend to tie bad bosses together? Is there any one thing that many, or most, have in common? Can bad boss activity be predicted, and prevented, or at least avoided? What can be concluded from reading these cases? A question that needs an answer, is how do these bad bosses get to be bosses? One clue, at least in some cases, is that the person has a personality change upon becoming a first time boss. The maligned employee(s) may often wonder why the company doesn't recognize the bad boss and do something. Sometimes it does. See if you agree with the action taken by the company in some cases.

Hopefully you will get some benefit from reading this book. It may provide guidance in avoiding or resolving conflicts in work situations.

It may help a stressed out employee to recognize a potentially difficult relationship in its early stages, and take some corrective action. It may help some good bosses become outstanding bosses. It may serve as a warning to some about-to-be bosses, as a caution to not change the personality that got them there. It may also provide some enjoyment in reading dramas of others' misfortunes and reactions in the workplace.

There really are Good Bosses
In Memory of Oliver Dale Wertz,
The Best Boss I ever had

As a young engineer I had been promoted to the job of Project Engineer where I had to manage people and technical projects. One of my first crises came in a meeting between engineering and drafting. A heated argument started between the drafting supervisor and myself. I won the argument. My boss, Dale Wertz happened to be attending the meeting. On the way out he commented to me, "I don't think that guy likes you." I responded with, "I don't care if he doesn't like me. He had better respect me. The tail is not going to wag the dog." Dale smiled and replied, "Yes, but your job sure would be easier if he liked you."

Even after we had both moved onto other jobs, I still relied on Dale for advice. This next example is important to the readers of this book. I was considering a major job change to another part of the country. Dale told me that over his years, that his family was the happiest when he was the happiest. We spend the most of our time on the job. We have invested a significant portion of our lives training and preparing and working. We can't afford to let a bad boss destroy our happiness.

Over the many years since, I have remembered and lived by Dale's words. I am very lucky to have had Dale's guidance early in my career.

Many years later I informally counseled a professional woman, a Ph.D. computer scientist. She didn't work for me. She didn't even work with me. I only knew her from exchanging pleasantries in the hallways over a couple of years. She just came into my office one day and unloaded on me the difficulties she was having with her boss. She was distraught. Having seen her in my office, Dr. Bill Premerlani, long time friend and colleague whose judgment I value (and who wrote the *Foreword* to this book), surmised the subject of our discussion. He told me, "People go into your office and come out feeling better than when they went in." (I learned later that Bill had suggested that she talk to me.)

During this writing, I talked with Bill on the phone, as we do often. He is now thinking of retirement after a brilliant career in engineering, having made many significant accomplishments in advancing the state of the art, and has authored several books. He asked questions about my own retirement. During the conversation he mentioned that he was now carrying on my mission of "ambassador of good will." I think perhaps the lessons taught me by Dale Wertz so many years before are still carrying forward. This makes me feel good. When Bill does retire, I'm sure he will have prepared someone else to carry on.

CASES

These cases stand alone and do not need to be read in any particular order.

Case 1

EGOMANIA:
The Over Egotistical Boss

Key Players:

- Howard: **Boss**
- Keith: Electrical Engineer
- Ian: Electrical Engineer

Synopsis:

The company had invested heavily in the field of micro-technology electronic circuit chips, called VLSI, or "very large scale integrated" circuit design. Microcircuits could be packaged on a chip with extreme density. Howard was the program manager of a design and development team. Keith and Ian were engineers, members of the team. They saw the need for what is known as an ASIC (Application Specific Integrated Circuit) chip for an application for one of the company's product lines. Howard was known as an aggressive manager, usually getting his way. Howard succeeded in obtaining company funds for himself, Keith and Ian to spend a month in intensive training in California at a company that, in cooperation with a prestigious university, had invented a new computer-aided chip design methodology.

A dozen teams from high tech companies attended the training course. Training was organized into instructional sessions in the mornings, and laboratory sessions in the afternoons, five days a week. Each brought a circuit design to be implemented and fabricated using the new micro-technology. The objective was to learn the methodology and take home a working micro-tech integrated circuit chip.

Keith and Ian designed a system using conventional means, to be converted to micro-technology. Early into the course Howard looked at Keith and Ian's design. Based on the circuit density possible using the micro-technology, Howard argued that three or four of the independent circuit units could be transferred onto a single chip, though much work would be required. He made arrangements for the lab facility to be open for his team at night and weekends. Keith and Ian argued that one circuit was enough to learn and demonstrate, but settled for two. Other teams looked on in awe at their fierce determination. It put the team's company into a good light as compared with the others. Howard relished the attention.

The team worked seven days and nights with little rest for the four-week duration. They met many difficulties. The new methodology still had flaws. When the final day came, the chip was not finished. All other teams had finished their simpler designs, and there was a time for celebration.

A wine tasting party was planned for the last night of the course. Howard's team did not attend the party, continuing to work. They worked all night without sleep. They were totally exhausted and did much arguing. They went from the lab, checked out of their motel and took the early morning flight home. They slept on the flight.

The course instructors promised to look at the chip design and see if they could fabricate it. The chip was finished and shipped to the team. It didn't work. It wasn't like it had failed some of its functions. It wouldn't perform any function. Keith and Ian were embarrassed, both at home and in front of the other participating teams. The company looked bad. Keith and Ian were quite angry.

What Went Right:

- Howard secured money to fund the training.
- The team learned the micro-tech design process, increasing their knowledge.

What Went Wrong:

- Project failed.

- Team disagreements.
- Long hours caused mistakes.
- Howard overestimated the capability of the team and new design methodology.
- Methodology was new and still had problems.
- Team had no working proof that they had learned anything in the course,
- Or that the new methodology even worked.
- They looked bad to their company management.
- They looked bad to the other participating companies.

Lessons Learned:

- The advanced design process training was the right thing to do.
- Recognize and beware of over egotistical boss.
- Engineering team should not concede to a manager known to be overly aggressive.
- A manager good at obtaining funds is not necessarily good at managing a design team.
- A manager should listen to his team.
- Risk should be assessed before pushing limits.
- It is better to bring in a working model on schedule and at cost, rather than an aggressive model that does not function.

Outcome:

Failure. (Fortunately, the team got a second chance and designed a micro-tech chip for another application. They learned from the earlier failure.)

Assessment of Management:

Howard was an aggressive and driving individual. Sometimes this is good -- not always. Howard managed to get company funds for the training course. The team had to study and learn the new technology, transform it into an integrated circuit and bring back a working chip.

There was time before the course for Keith and Ian to design a functional system and do computer simulations to be confident of the design. They informed Howard of their progress, but never got into the details. They had a count of the number of circuit components, but did not know how much real estate the design and wiring would take on the chip. While the technology allowed a very large number of components per unit area, the layout of the circuit with its wiring is very complex. Howard trusted that Keith and Ian had designed a functionally correct system, evidenced by computer simulation.

Howard didn't listen to their advice about trying to stuff too much circuitry on their first experience. He accused them of not putting forth enough effort. When the work could not be finished, Keith and Ian accused Howard of forcing a wrong decision. Howard never admitted a mistake. It's not known what he told his management. Howard was good at selling his project, but not realistic in implementation. He wanted to be the best.

What would you do if you were in Keith's/Ian's positions?

- Would you have a confrontation with Howard?
- Would you complain to higher management?
- Could you reconcile Howard's bad management points with his good?
- Would you attempt another design using the micro-technology you had learned?
- With Howard as leader?
- Other?

Case 2

GLASS CEILING:
Discrimination and Under the Table Hiring

Key Players:

- Earl: **Boss**
- Jeremy: **Boss' Boss**
- Josh: Engineer
- Becky: Computer Scientist

Synopsis:

The company had a central facility for research and development (R&D), the function of which was to discover, invent, and develop technologies that would transition to products for the company's businesses. The center was divided into functional areas such as physics, chemistry, engineering, etc., plus a number of supporting organizations. The engineering division included an Information Technology Laboratory (ITL) made up of engineers and computer scientists. The computer scientists all had advanced degrees in computer science. The engineers also had advanced degrees and had training and experience in computer science as well as engineering.

The ITL was subdivided among what were known as programs with four program managers reporting to the ITL Manager. The engineers were all men, but the computer scientists were about evenly divided between women and men. The four program managers were men. Josh was an engineer and Becky was a computer scientist, both reporting to different program managers.

The ITL had been without a permanent manager for a number of months since the manager's transfer to another company location. The higher manager, Jeremy, had told the ITL members to use a democratic process and find a manager from outside the company. During the interim, Jeremy appointed one of the four male program managers to double duty acting as ITL Manager.

Human Resources (HR) brought in four candidates from outside the company for interviews. The ITL employees were considered individual contributors, worked autonomously, didn't care much who was manager, within reasonable limits. Most thought that Jeremy, acting with HR assistance and with their advice, should hire a new ITL manager, preferably from within the company. As with all employment candidates, each candidate was given the stage to sell himself to the company. Then he progressed to individual interviews. The majority rejected all of the four candidates because the engineers and computer scientists couldn't agree. Jeremy was displeased and issued a mandate that someone be hired.

A woman computer scientist in the ITL, Becky, began a campaign to get her favorite candidate, number 4, accepted. She spoke to all ITL members and made a case for hiring candidate number 4, Earl, who held a Ph.D. in her specialty field of computer science. He showed no credibility in engineering. He claimed to have management experience and good contacts with Government funding sources. His claims later turned out to be untrue, however. He also turned out to be an ineffective manager. But, again, the ITL members didn't seem to care.

ITL members learned later that Becky and Earl had known each other in a previous business relationship, and rumors began that they had entered into a pact. The word spread through the ITL. She would get him "elected" as the ITL Manager if he, in turn, would then promote her to program manager. Recommendation was made to Jeremy, and Earl was hired.

As time went by it was noticed that Becky and Earl were spending large amounts of time together and detected favoritism in such things as funding allocations. Josh and the other engineers were to joke about Earl and his "girlfriend", Becky.

Becky made it publicly known that she wanted a promotion to program manager. Becky had such influence that it was joked that she was running the ITL. Josh and other individual contributors felt they and their projects were not getting fair attention from Earl because of his time spent with Becky. Clearly Becky had a hold on Earl. Josh also saw that total support was going to the computer science projects and none for engineering projects.

Josh was particularly annoyed with the situation because he was trying to build his own engineering program and needed Earl's attention. He blamed Becky for taking Earl's time and other resources, and blamed Earl for not being able to handle the situation.

But as time went by, hostility began to show between Earl and Becky. The reason was simple. Earl did not promote Becky to program manager. This relationship caused even more neglect of the other members of the ITL. Josh's hostility toward Earl grew as a result. Hostility toward Becky grew also.

After two years had gone by, Becky left the company. She left behind a scathing letter to HR spelling out her dissatisfaction. She went on to be interviewed by a popular working women's magazine. She related her side of the story, complaining about the "glass ceiling" in the company that prevented women from becoming managers. She claimed that Earl was guilty of supporting that concept.

Wikipedia defines glass ceilings as follows: "The term glass ceiling refers to situations where the advancement of a person within the hierarchy of an organization is limited. Limitation is normally based upon some form of discrimination, most commonly gender and race. This situation is referred to as a 'ceiling' as there is a limitation blocking upward advancement, and 'glass' (transparent) because the limitation is not immediately apparent and is normally an unwritten and unofficial policy. The 'glass ceiling' is distinguished from formal barriers to advancement, such as education or experience requirements."

Much has been written about the "glass ceiling", especially as it relates to women in business. It is easy to find many references for further study.

Becky wasn't finished with the company. She filed a lawsuit based on the "glass ceiling" concept of discriminating against women. After some time the lawsuit was settled out of court. The terms of the settlement were not made public.

It took another year, but Earl was fired. A departmental reorganization caused the ITL to be merged with another laboratory, with a redistribution of the members.

What Went Right:

- A new manager, Earl was hired. This satisfied Jeremy and the higher management.
- The new manager, Earl, was eventually fired. That satisfied the engineers.

What Went Wrong:

- The higher level manager, Jeremy, shirked his duty by not selecting and hiring a new manager for the ITL.
- The new manager, Earl, did not promote the woman computer scientist.
- A previously productive employee, the computer scientist, Becky, left the company.
- A lawsuit resulted.
- The company received bad publicity when Becky was interviewed by a popular working women's magazine. She accused the manager and the company of practicing the "glass ceiling" philosophy of denying management positions to women.
- Earl was asked to leave because of a combination of incompetence and the trouble he caused.
- Again the ITL was without a manager. This time the ITL was merged with another laboratory.
- Josh's project was discontinued.

Lessons Learned:

- The responsible manager should not delegate to the (managed) group the democratic process of hiring the group's manager.
- Deceitful, unethical agreements in hiring can have negative results.
- Apathy by the technical group in selecting one's boss can be disastrous.
- Infighting should be recognized early and dealt with accordingly.

Outcome:

An unqualified manager was hired. Major employee discontent resulted. Eventually he was fired. The ITL, left in disarray, was merged with another organization. The female employee, Becky, left the company, provided a personal interview for a popular women's magazine accusing the company of "glass ceiling" practices. Then she filed a gender discrimination lawsuit, which was settled out of court. Josh's project was disrupted by all the in-fighting and was discontinued.

Assessment of Management:

This case presents a compound problem. There are levels of complications. The members of the organization were happy doing what they were doing, and didn't want to be involved in selecting their own leader. This may be attributed to the fact that the group was made up of a mix of engineers and computer scientists with different interests. The hiring manager, Jeremy, thought he was being nice by allowing the members of the unit to select their own manager. He, in fact, was shirking his duty as a manager.

To hire a manager from outside the company should have called for special circumstances. This is generally covered by company procedure. No special circumstances here are known. After all, the ITL management job was being done in the interim by one of the lower level program managers, while he was continuing to perform in his own job. It may have been appropriate to promote the acting manager to the higher level. Then replace him from within the ranks. Becky clearly wanted the job. Becky might have been replaced in her computer scientist position without any rifts within the organization.

Becky may or may not have been qualified for the job of program manager. In all probability Earl could not promote Becky because a new program would have to be started. Further, he would have to get approval from his higher management, Jeremy. Jeremy had already demonstrated his lack of competence. Earl could not, or at least did not, keep his end of the deal with Becky, if in fact there was a deal.

On the surface there was nothing wrong with Becky's recommendation of Earl for the job. Her prior relationship with Earl, of course, should have been revealed in the beginning. It was unethical, however, to have made an under the table deal. The deal, of course, could not be binding.

Whether there was gender discrimination is questionable. In this case the "glass ceiling" may or may not have existed. As for Becky's claim, it could not be substantiated because during the time involved, no men were promoted to program manager either. The way things were handled triggered an organization meltdown.

How would you define the problem?

- Who acted unethically?
- Who suffered most from this fiasco?
- Was the company lacking in procedure to cover hiring managers?
- Why do you think the higher management wanted an outsider?
- Did the higher management act improperly? Did HR?
- Did the lawsuit have merit, or was it a grudge against Earl?
- Should Earl have been fired? Or should he have ever been hired?
- Did Becky experience the effect of the "glass ceiling"?
- Should Josh have done anything? If so, what?
- What would you have done if you were in Josh's position?

Case 3

PLEASE LET GO:
The Boss Who Wouldn't Delegate

Key Players:

- Landon: **Boss**
- Terry: New Manager reporting to Landon.

Synopsis:

The Company for a number of years had been developing new technology in alternate electrical power generation (for example, wind power). At the same time it was well known that China was working on several power projects getting ready for the forthcoming Summer Olympics of 2008. A few years earlier China had also entered into the World Trade Organization (WTO). Chinese companies could become formidable competitors, could be big customers, or collaborators for mutual benefit.

Landon was a first level manager of an Internationally diversified engineering program. Landon had eight engineers, two technicians and two programmers and an administrative assistant as direct reports. There was an opportunity for Landon's engineering program to expand Internationally. Landon and his engineers had started discussions of a joint venture with a power company in Beijing, China.

Just then, Landon was promoted to a higher management level position. In the new position Landon would have to find a replacement for himself, and would take on four more programs. In effect he would have five first level managers reporting to him in his new job.

Terry was an engineer in another program comparable to that previously managed by Landon. Terry was several years younger than Landon, and had recently completed the requirements and had received the MBA degree. Terry considered himself on a fast track for management, and it appeared that Landon might be also. Terry's current manager was not, as he had held the same management position for several years, was technically obsolete and appeared to be going nowhere in management. Terry's boss seemed to be doing an all right job in his current position, and no one saw any need for him to change. Terry was facing an obstacle. In order to stay with the company and get a promotion to a management level, he had to move out of his present operation. Terry had a strong resume that showed progress in all previous work. Further, he had experience working with China and seemed a qualified successor to Landon's old job.

Terry applied for Landon's previous job, got the job and in doing so, he reported to Landon in Landon's new job. In turn, Terry inherited the team that had previously reported to Landon. Further, it was his understanding that he would be taking over the project that was expected to grow into a joint venture with the power company in China. Terry considered his transfer and promotion to be a great opportunity. Landon's new job would require him to oversee Terry's program as well as four other programs.

Terry began a series of meetings with his new subordinates to learn the details of the alternate power generation program. After a short time he learned that Landon was circumventing him and discussing program details with the subordinates as though no management change had ever occurred. He further learned that Landon was continuing to communicate directly with the Chinese power company. Terry learned of instances of email involving decisions whereas he had not been on distribution. When he reported something significant to Landon, he found that Landon already knew, and in some cases had taken action without his knowledge. Terry hesitated to communicate with the Chinese power company officials for fear of duplication or contradiction of Landon's actions. Terry's own planning seemed to be wasted. Little progress was being made in developing the proposal for a joint venture with the Chinese company. Terry sensed that things were going terribly wrong.

What Went Right:

- Both Terry and Landon received managerial promotions.
- Both managers were focused on making the joint venture work.

What Went Wrong:

- Landon was not willing to relinquish control and turn over the project to Terry.
- Landon circumvented Terry in regard to all matters.
- Landon devoted almost all of his time to Terry's program.
- Other programs under Landon's control suffered because of Landon's neglect.
- The proposed joint venture began to show signs of failure.
- The project did not improve the resume of either manager.

Lessons Learned:

- A manager must delegate.
- A manager should not do the work of subordinates.
- On promotion to a higher level, a manager should let go of his old job.
- A second level (or higher) manager must use leverage through subordinate managers.

Outcome:

The program struggled along inefficiently and finally failed. Both managers eventually left the company.

Assessment of Management:

The reluctance of Landon to relinquish control is not that unusual, however these situations usually work themselves out if given time. Often technical contributors are promoted to management without any management training or experience. Landon, while a first level manager, was still close to the technical action. His promotion to the next higher level moved him further away from the action. It is also possible that he feared he would lose credit for work he had started, and the credit would go to the finisher.

A person may be confident in his capabilities in his present job, but wants a promotion for any number or reasons, including money and power. Oftentimes the manager considers his technical expertise to be his security blanket. But he realizes that the longer he stays away from the technical work, the harder it becomes for him to go back. He finds himself technically obsolete. Landon was transferred into a management position without adequate training. On the other hand, Terry had been preparing himself by evidence of his MBA degree.

The resulting situation caused hardships for all the employees concerned. Terry was promoted based on his potential. Landon was promoted based on the perceived value of his being able to hit the ground running in his new job. Looking back, it may have been better for Terry to have skipped a level and moved directly into the job for which Landon had been promoted. Landon could have been allowed to complete the project he had started, where he could have demonstrated his readiness for promotion to higher management. The situation was made more complicated by the fact that the project involved dealing with a foreign company. Both managers had some experience working with the Eastern business culture, which is clearly different from their own business culture. Under the circumstances, the project might have been predicted to fail.

What was the problem?

What would you do if you were in Terry's position?

- Nothing?
- Would you go to higher management?
- Would you go to HR?
- Would you discuss your concerns with Landon?

- Would you ignore Landon's interference and go ahead with the foreign company?
- Would you look for another job?
- Would you blame Landon for the failure of the joint venture?
- Other?

How could the project have been saved?

Case 4

SEE NO EVIL:
The Boss who looked the other way

Key Players:

- David: **Boss**
- Patrick: Electrical Engineer

Synopsis:

Patrick was a senior engineer who reported to David, a manager who had many years of experience as both engineer and engineering manager, as well as many years with the company. Patrick was spending a considerable amount of time away from the home office, as leader of a team of engineers, technicians and computer programmers at a remote field site. Patrick was pretty much autonomous in his work of testing a new hardware and software system. He had periodic meetings with David on his trips back home. They usually talked about budgets, manpower and schedules, and any problems that Patrick might have in the field. Patrick took pride in his ability to handle problems in the field without any assistance from his boss, David.

The work in the field involved working inside an electric power distribution substation near high voltages, a very hazardous situation. A mistake could cause serious injury, or death. There were strict rules, as well as common sense, that there must never be allowed only one person inside the field site. On one occasion Patrick told David that in order to meet a milestone in his schedule, he had had to violate the rule, and allowed himself to work alone in the substation. David quickly replied, "Don't tell me that."

Patrick went about his business, and sometime later at another meeting back at the home office, Patrick said he could not make the next contract milestone unless he had additional funding. David said the funding was fixed and Patrick would have to solve the problem in some other way. Schedule is of primary importance. Patrick said that the only way he knew to do that would be to skip some of the required tests. Again David replied, "Don't tell me how you do it". Patrick decided to assume the risk and skipped over some of the tests.

As time went by, there were other situations where corners had to be cut to meet schedule and budget. David's response was the same, "Don't tell me. I don't want to know." At lunch one day Patrick confided with an engineering associate who also reported to David. His friend told him that David had treated him the same way, and gave an example about what might have been an infringement on another company's patent. He went on to say that David had a talent for distancing himself from questionable, unethical and possibly illegal activities. In Patrick's situation there may have been physically dangerous circumstances. If such activities became known, or if disaster should occur, David could declare or testify that he wasn't told.

What Went Right:

- Patrick and his team accomplished the technical objectives of the project.
- The project accomplishments were transitioned into a prototype for a new product as originally planned.
- The risks paid off.

What Went Wrong:

- The project team took risks that flirted with disaster.
- The boss isolated himself from the risk.
- The boss' motives served only himself.

Lessons Learned:

- Identify risks, and assess probability of successful outcomes or failures.
- Known risks should be assessed in terms of the magnitude of possible loss.
- Do intense planning to reduce risk.
- No risk should ever be taken where one's safety is endangered.
- Risk is not always shared.
- Inform the boss of risks and consequences.
- The boss with David's philosophy cannot be depended upon.
- One should think very seriously about supporting a non-supportive boss.
- Keep good records.

Outcome:

Project finished successfully. Fortunately, the risks paid off.

Management Assessment:

Both Patrick and David understood the company's emphasis on schedule and budget. Of most importance is the schedule. All employees knew the facetious saying, "You may not have enough time to get it right the first time, but you always have enough time to fix it." David is a manager who presses for results. He wants to get the credit, but not the blame. He is likely following a business culture that originates at the highest levels within the company. He has worked for the company for many years. He is known as "a survivor."

David could, however, share in the risk, and perhaps reduce the risk simply by becoming more involved in the planning, rather than pushing others for results. Also, the risks may be of such consequence that should never be taken. An example would be working alone in a high voltage environment. A prudent manager would assess the risk and then take action. His actions could not only be costly to the company, but could actually endanger the lives of employees.

A manager can delegate authority, such as the authority to accept risks on the job, but cannot delegate responsibility. Turning a deaf ear does not necessarily shift the blame if things go wrong. Rather, it is a show of incompetence in a manager. The manager has to ask several questions: What are the risks? How can the risk be reduced or eliminated? What are the possible outcomes? What risks are worth taking, and what risks can never be taken under any circumstances?

David was following a course such as those investigated within the U.S. Government in Washington, that is, who knew what and when? In the industry there are what are known as CYA letters (cover your ass, ref. Wikipedia). If Patrick put his planned actions in writing, then David would be placed in a compromising position. However, this might put Patrick's job in jeopardy, thereby pitting one risk against another. In any case, Patrick should keep an accurate daily log of his activities on the job and his interactions with his boss.

What is the problem?

What would you do if you were in Patrick's position?

- Would you tell David about the risks?
- Would you force a discussion of risks with David?
- Would you refuse to take certain risks for the sake of schedule and budget?

Would you look for another job?

Case 5

SHADE of GRAY:
The Case of the Boss' Kickback

Key Players:

- George: The **Boss**
- Harvey: Lead Engineer
- Daniel: Lab Technician
- Bidder No.1
- Bidder No.2
- Bidder No.3

Synopsis:

The company had been awarded a Government contract to design, develop and test a series of equipment to be used in an aerospace application. In order to carry out the provisions of the contract the company had to spend a considerable amount of money for new computers and various specialized test equipment for the laboratory. The computers were fairly simple to purchase, as the supplier proposing the equivalent computers at the lowest price would win the subcontract. The specialized test equipment had to be designed with special requirements and interfaces, and the lab facility required modifications.

George was the manager with responsibility for the Government contract, as well as for the laboratory. Harvey, an engineer, and Daniel, a lab technician, were assigned the responsibility for producing a specification for the test equipment and soliciting competitive bids. They spent the first month developing a specification. They allowed considerable flexibility to take into account innovative designs and the long-term benefits versus cost.

When competing bids came in, the three most favorable bidders were invited to come into the plant and make presentations of their proposals. In addition to Harvey and Daniel, George and other laboratory people attended these presentations that were scheduled about a week apart. Following each presentation Harvey, Daniel and George were invited to lunch by the respective bidder reps. They all accepted. Such had been done on other occasions, and they felt that they treated each rep the same way and no favoritism was shown. Nothing was done that was not legal, at least as far as they knew. However, each of the three bidders began calling Harvey fairly frequently. Harvey and Daniel evaluated the proposals technically, and decided that all three proposals met the requirements of the specification. They recommended Bidder No.3, the low bidder. They would document their evaluation and tell George their decision.

In the meantime, Bidder No.2 requested another visit. Harvey and No.2 had a short meeting. Harvey didn't remember exactly what was said, but he left confused, as thinking that No.2 had, in a round about way, offered him an incentive. Since he wasn't sure, he didn't tell anyone, not even Daniel.

A few days later Harvey and Daniel recommended No.3 to George. George recommended that they reconsider No.2, "Well, I just think we will be better satisfied with No.2's proposed equipment, and they offer better service." When reminded that No.2 was not the low bidder, he said, "I'll write the justification letter to the purchasing office, or maybe we can get No.2 to lower the bid."

Harvey discussed the situation with Daniel. Harvey confided with Daniel that No. 2 hinted that he wanted to make an "under the table deal". Daniel shared with Harvey the suspicion that George had entered into a side deal with Bidder No.2. They didn't know what to do.

They decided to defer to the wishes of the boss and proceeded with the paperwork to purchase from Bidder No.2. Bidder No. 2 was awarded the subcontract. Relations between them and George became somewhat strained. Both Harvey and Daniel believed strongly that George had taken a bribe from Bidder No.2.

What Went Right:

- Harvey and Daniel accomplished the purpose by buying equipment that would suit the laboratory needs.

What Went Wrong:

- The boss went against the recommendation of his expert people who set the standards and evaluated the responses.
- The boss may have done something unethical or illegal.
- The boss's action caused strained relationships with Harvey and Daniel.
- Harvey and Daniel believed the company over paid for the equipment. The cost was passed on to the Government agency in accordance with the contract.

Lessons Learned:

- Try to know what to do in advance in case of integrity issues.
- Communicate closely with the boss. Know what each is going to do.
- In the words of President Ronald Reagan in the last days of the Cold War, "Trust, but verify."
- Include your procurement manager, or other representative, in meetings with vendors.
- Keep detailed records of all activities.

Outcome:

Project was a success, but personal relations were harmed.

Management Assessment:

The equipment procurement team did a good job of developing a specification for the needed equipment. They got a sufficient number of bids to assure the specifications were reasonable and the requirements could be satisfied, and within the budget.

It was inappropriate for the boss to have discussions with one of the bidders without Harvey's and Daniel's knowledge. It is not known how the meeting was initiated, or if the boss had discussions with the other two bidders. In a cost-reimbursable type contract, the Government would reimburse the company for certain agreed upon expenditures. The action of the boss may have been illegal. Harvey and Daniel felt strongly that George took a kickback. The subcontract should have been awarded to the lowest qualified bidder, which was No.3.

If bidders No.1 and No.3 should have become aware that No.2 was given special consideration, then they would have reason to complain. Bribes are difficult to prove, but it is not likely that the boss could be effective in his relations with Harvey and Daniel in the future.

Harvey and Daniel were taking a risk no matter what they were to do. If they spoke out and if they turned out to be wrong, a severe injustice would have been done. Further, they would jeopardize their jobs. On the other hand, if they kept quiet, one of at least two things could happen. They could continue and implement the plan with Bidder No. 2, and live with the damage already done with their relations with George. Or, in the worst case, George's actions, if in fact illegal, could be exposed and they could be accused as accomplices.

Their best bet might be to keep detailed logs of all activities during the course of the procurement action. Since distrust had already been established, it would be well to continue the permanent ledger. Such a strategy is sometimes known as a CYA (cover your ass) document.

What was the problem?

What would you do if you were in the position of Harvey or Daniel?

- Nothing?
- Would you go to higher management?
- Would you go to HR?
- Would you discuss with each other?
- Would you discuss with George?
- Would you confront Bidder No.2?

- ■ Other?
- ■ What are your risks in whatever you do?
- ■ What are the company's risks if Harvey and Daniel's suspicions were true?

Case 6

DID WHAT?
The No Results Boss

Key Players:

- Roy: **Boss**
- Oliver: Engineer
- Lee: Engineer

Synopsis:

Oliver and Lee were engineers in a research environment, who along with other engineers and scientists reported to a manager named Roy. This organization had been together for about four years, though most worked on individual projects. Oliver and Lee worked closely together and shared technical theories. They enjoyed their work, found the projects to be interesting and challenging. They worked at their own pace, and gave periodic presentations to Roy and the other members of his staff. The others did likewise. Over the four years, they had worked on four different projects. Early each year budgets were approved for the coming year.

One January morning Oliver and Lee were having coffee. The conversation went something like this: Lee said, "Oliver, you know there is something that we are learning from working for Roy. We don't ever have to finish a project, or ever deliver anything. Somehow he gets money approved for us to go on working. We enjoy the projects, we learn something, and we actually accomplish something, but it all ends without anyone getting any benefit from our work. It's discouraging."

Lee went on to say, "This past year we explored new algorithms for simplifying programming of parallel computing. We made significant advancements, but no product department wanted to continue it. Then, the year before we developed a new concept related to medical imaging that would greatly reduce costs. We were led to believe that smaller hospitals wanted less expensive systems. The medical systems department didn't think the lower cost system would sell."

"Yes", Oliver replied. "And I don't like it. We aren't getting any patents or papers, and we aren't advancing our careers. The projects just don't go anywhere. I don't understand why our funding sources let Roy get away with it. I asked Roy if I could at least write a technical paper on the last project before I went on to the next. Roy refused my request, saying that the funding for the old project had stopped. He said I could not charge the new funding to the old project. That left me as if I had not worked on the previous project at all. "

Lee said, "I'll tell you how he gets the projects funded. The product business departments are told by corporate headquarters to hand over part of their profits for pure research. We get free money without accountability. It's not fair to the funding businesses or to the stockholders, or to us. To Roy it seems to be fun and games. He gets to manage an organization and gets highly paid for it."

Oliver said, "We don't finish anything. We have got to do something about it. We aren't getting anything of accomplishment to put on our resumes. Sooner or later this is going to have to end, and we'll be in trouble looking for another job."

What Went Right:

- Project funding was renewed at the beginning of each year.
- The engineering projects ran smoothly up until funding stopped.
- Then there were other projects to work on with new funding.
- The engineers received annual cost-of-living salary increases.

What Went Wrong:

- The engineers believed they were in dead-end jobs.
- There were no tangible results of their work.
- There were no papers or patents.

- The engineers had no work "results" for their resumes.
- Their futures seemed uncertain.
- Morale went down.

Lessons Learned:

- Set goals and objectives.
- Deliver periodic results.
- Make sure that what you do is worthy of an entry on your resume.
- Stay alert to signs that the project is headed to a dead end.
- Plan ahead accordingly.

Outcome:

One by one the employees left Roy's organization, until it finally dissolved into another organization.

Assessment of Management:

The manager seemed to feel that his only obligation was to keep his employees employed. He did not seem to realize that the highly trained and skilled employees wanted tangible results from their work. They felt that their work was all being wasted, and that there was no opportunity for advancement. The manager allowed the morale to sink low. The situation was like the cliché that "a woodchopper who is paid by the hour still wants a sharp axe".

Roy seemed to view the work as purely academic. However, if that were the case, he should have encouraged papers and patents. That would have at least provided a record and some personal satisfaction. With records, projects not now ready for the market, for whatever reasons, could be retrieved and built upon at later times.

Oliver and Lee became, at least temporarily, complacent in their jobs. However, after a long enough period of time, they decided that this complacency must come to an end. They sought accomplishment and recognition of accomplishment. Their logical recourse was to transfer to other jobs with different management.

What do you think was the problem?

What would you do if you were in Oliver's or Lee's position?

- Nothing? Accept the situation and continue?
- Would you try to resolve issues with Roy?
- Would you go to Roy's boss?
- Would you look for another job?
- Other?

Case 7

WHISTLE BLOWER:
The Boss Who Got Caught

Key Players:

- Joe: **Boss**
- Phil: Lead Engineer

Synopsis:

Phil was the lead engineer on a project that was funded by the U.S. Government. Phil and his project team reported to Joe who had financial responsibility.

The project was a multi-phased, multi-year project. The phases were for 1) a phase of study for feasibility, 2) a phase to design and test a prototype, and 3) a phase to manufacture and deliver a quantity of the resulting products. The project team was composed of six people, engineers, technicians and programmers working full time. The beginning of each new phase was contingent on successful completion and evaluation of the preceding phase.

The project funding was a cost reimbursable and fixed fee type, which means that it was a high-risk project with the Government absorbing the risks. The Government paid for labor and materials and paid a negotiated fee, or profit, to the company. The contract was known as CPFF (Cost Plus Fixed Fee, meaning the Government would pay all costs incurred and the company's profit, ie., fee, was negotiated and fixed), one of several contract types used by the Government. The end of the year was approaching, and the project was behind schedule and the authorized funding would be running out. Negotiations had been underway for funding to continue on to the next phase of the project.

At the beginning of the next year Joe informed Phil that funding for the current phase had run out and he and the team should start charging their time and materials to the funding account authorized and set up for the next phase. After all, it was a continuation of the same project, and the team should continue working toward the completion of the current phase. Upon completion, the team would then transition smoothly to the next phase.

All was well except the practice of charging and billing for a later contract, and applying the funds toward the completion of the previous project is illegal. This same logic would apply to any business that bills for labor by the hours worked on a project. It's like an attorney billing a client for work done for another client. Phil knew that such charging was illegal.

Phil and his team had to work much overtime without pay to bring the project up to the point where a smooth transition could be made into the next phase. The team members were very unhappy because they had to work extra hours without pay because of factors over which they had no control.

What Went Right:

■ The project team did good work.

What Went Wrong:

■ The project time and costs were underestimated.
■ The project got behind schedule.
■ A phase of the project ran out of money.
■ Phil and Joe did not communicate well, about work progress and depleting funds.
■ The project team members were angry to have to work overtime without pay.
■ The manager, Joe, instructed his employees to charge their time to the wrong contract.
■ Phil and the project team broke the law by following Joe's instructions.

Lessons Learned:

- Need to learn how to estimate time and costs more accurately.
- Build in contingencies to take care of project overruns.
- Raise a flag as soon as you know the project may not make its scheduled milestones.
- Weigh the alternatives carefully.
- Assess the risks of not remaining within budget.
- Develop a back up plan.
- Don't be a party to a cover up.

Outcome:

The project continued with unhappy people and people running the risk of being caught in illegal activities.

Assessment of Management:

What Joe did is what embezzlers do before getting caught. They borrow ahead with intentions of paying back the funds. Unfortunately, many times they cannot pay back the "borrowed" funds, and they get in deeper and get caught. Once the borrowing has begun, it is too late to come clean.

Joe should have reported to the Government funding agency that the project was behind schedule, and then proposed a plan to get back on track. Once mischarging had begun, there was no easy way out. The Government knew there was technical and financial risk involved, as was the reason for the cost reimbursable contract. If the work had been of a nature that it could have been done without risk, the contract would have been a firm fixed price, known as FFP. That is like saying that the company had done the required work many times before. Clearly that was not the case here.

Phil had a very risky dilemma. He could go along with mischarging, which is fraud, or he could refuse. Refusal could cost him his job, as he would not have any funds to which he could charge his time. To go along with the mischarging, he ran the risk of getting caught and suffering the consequences of loss of job plus legal action. Though his risk of the latter is less than that of his boss, Joe, who authorized and directed the financial dealings.

As another alternative, Phil could have become a whistle blower. However, whistle blowers generally lose on all accounts. This is especially true when going against a big company, such as in Phil's case. Once a person is labeled a whistle blower, he/she is never trusted again. To make the problem many times worse is the fact that the Government some years before had caught another department of the company in the same activity. The penalty was quite severe in terms of monetary fines, and the company had installed checks to prevent it from happening again. Several people had been fired. Fortunately no one went to jail. Many people felt this was part of the penalty agreement with the Government. However, after fair warning, another infraction might be different.

What do you think was the problem?

What would you do if you were in Phil's position?

- ■ Nothing?
- ■ Would you try to argue the issue with Joe?
- ■ Would you go to higher management?
- ■ Would you go to HR?
- ■ Would you look for another job?
- ■ Would you become a whistle blower?
- ■ Other?

Case 8

WINNER TAKE ALL:
The Bosses' Power Struggle

Key Players:

- Eddie: **First Boss**
- Donald: **Second Boss**
- Jack: Design Engineer on project team

Synopsis:

An engineering team was formed in the company's Philadelphia plant to develop a new digital concept in electric power utility applications. The project team was assembled and led by Eddie who had many years experience in power applications. Eddie recruited Jack from another department location for his expertise in digital equipment design. A software engineer from the company's computer department joined the team to lead software development. Several others were brought together from various company components to complete the team. Eddie had created relationships with other company components with business interests, power utility companies in three states that provided funding and expert advisors, and a power utility company in a Midwestern state to provide a power distribution substation for online testing. Another source of funding and expert advice was an electric power research institute, a membership organization that contracts for research to benefit all member utility companies.

Eddie's vision was to start a new product line and a new company business department, with the team members assured management jobs. Eddie was innovative and was highly respected by his peers, his team, the power utility company sponsors and the funding agency.

The multi-year project was organized in three phases. The first was to study the problem, conceptualize, design and build a prototype system. This was done in Philadelphia at the company department expected to gain the most benefit. The second phase was to move the system into a power environment provided by a municipal utility in another state for extensive testing. The third was planned to take the new products to the marketplace.

The first phase was completed successfully in two years. Then when the second phase was into its second year, corporate headquarters made a decision to consolidate research and development projects from various components of the company into one location in another state. Eddie, Jack and the whole project team were moved accordingly.

The new command immediately appointed its own manager, a man named Donald, to head the project. Eddie and the project team assumed that Eddie would report to Donald. The project team already knew Donald from his attendance at project reviews from time to time. It soon became clear that Donald expected to act as project manager for the project, displacing Eddie, though no such formal announcement was ever made. Eddie, who had defined the project, brought the team together, secured funding and outside participation, was relegated to a lesser position. Because he had the knowledge and team's trust he continued to do the same job, but without the title and defined authority he once had. Jack and the rest of the team continued working as if no change had taken place. They were just in a new location. But soon, animosity became apparent between Eddie and new manager Donald.

Eddie took a vacation, during which time Donald visited the field testing site where Jack and the team were spending most of their time. Donald asked questions about the ongoing work and who was doing what. He wanted to know what job Eddie was doing. When told that Eddie was project leader and systems engineer, Donald exclaimed, "But that's my job now!" He then asked, "Why wasn't Eddie doing the digital design?" Jack explained that Eddie was doing the systems engineering, and that all on the team were specialists in different areas. Jack, himself was doing the digital hardware design. Donald then said he would have to appraise Eddie's work performance as a digital hardware designer, and it wouldn't be good. Jack objected to that, but to no avail. Jack also felt that the design was his job, and he knew that Eddie's strengths were elsewhere. Jack felt threatened by Donald. He had no idea where Donald's strengths were. He quickly became concerned that Donald would rearrange jobs and put the project and everyone's job in jeopardy.

Jack, and also other team members, were confused as to whom they should report. They felt the logical thing was to report to their de facto leader the same as in the past. Eddie knew the ins and outs of the project and had good relations with outside participants and funding sources. However, Donald was the assigned manager and was given apparent authority accordingly. No formal announcement of the hierarchy of the management was ever issued. No technical management instructions ever came from Donald. Further, Donald never participated in any technical meetings of the group. But, Donald was the boss who would be writing performance appraisals. Performance appraisals converted directly into salary actions.

On his return from vacation Eddie confided to Jack that he was considering going to Donald's boss with an ultimatum, that he or Donald should bow out. Donald simply was not needed. Jack advised against that, hoping that the problem would go away. Jack also felt that Eddie would lose, that they were now in Donald's territory. Jack could tell that Eddie was experiencing extraordinary stress.

After several weeks Eddie developed a medical problem and checked into a hospital. It was winter. He told the team he had slipped on ice and was recovering. He missed several days of work.

Finally, back at the new home office, the problem came to a head, and Eddie was asked to leave. Because of the bad appraisal given him by Donald, he was unable to find another job within the company. He ended up getting a job with the nonprofit organization that was helping to fund his (former) project. He could have sabotaged the project, but he didn't. The project continued for another two years to completion. After project completion, a new business venture was started in a new location in Pennsylvania, somewhat like Eddie's original plan. No project team member was asked to participate. The team members all went on separately to other projects. The software engineer left the company, and the remaining software development was outsourced. Donald published papers on the project and received a promotion.

What Went Right:

- The team accomplished the technical objectives of the project.
- The team stuck it out under adverse conditions.
- The project accomplishments were turned into a business venture as planned.

What Went Wrong:

- Transfer of the project from one company component to another did not go smoothly.
- A bitter fight ensued between the original manager and the newly appointed manager.
- The original manager was demoted, and undoubtedly was driven into a severe state of depression.
- The team whose members did the work got little credit.
- The original manager was eventually fired.
- The wrong person got promoted.

Lessons Learned:

- Understand the business culture of the new assignment in advance of a transfer.
- Negotiate roles before making a department change.
- When a project changes departments, don't try to unseat the manager appointed by the receiving company department. It won't work.
- Management can be unfair and greedy.
- Company politics are stronger than technical project expertise.

Outcome:

The project was considered a success. A new business was started in a new location. The team was dispersed to other projects. The company benefited, but the team did not reap the planned benefits.

Assessment of Management:

Many times decisions made at the corporate level are not in the best interest of the people in the business components. Even though the company had a central corporate research and development center, by far the most research and development work was done by the business departments to satisfy their own needs. The central R&D would apply mostly to research with unknown, or many, applications to satisfy more than one business' product needs.

One thing that may have been bad for the project was its long duration. In that time it is common for many things to change in a large company, for example, the economy, sources of funding, the needs for the project, and the people.

It's hard to imagine any decisions at the corporate level would be made for any reason other than money. In the overall scheme it may have made sense to consolidate many projects into one place to take advantage of a large pool of many more talents in a stable environment. On the receiving end, the managers would want to know what is in it for them to gain a project with its team of people. It gave Donald, the resident manager, a management job at the expense of a more qualified Eddie, who came with the project. It was immediately a power struggle.

Eddie appeared to have been a victim of the system. Eddie's medical problem was likely stress related as the result of losing control of the innovative project he had created. Depression was not a subject to be discussed by technical people. He suffered a great loss. He had been moved into a hostile business culture where Donald, a member of a cutthroat culture, was an opportunist with a large ego, and had no regard for the people on whom he stepped.

While Eddie suffered the most, Jack and the other team members worked under great stress. The project itself was placed in jeopardy of failure. Donald's responsibility did not seem to go with his authority. He seemed to exercise his authority, and yet wanted to shirk the accompanying responsibility.

The company considered the project a success, but none of the project team continued with the project as it turned into a new product line with its own business department. Project team members could all be considered casualties of a company philosophy passed down by corporate headquarters. That is to say, that they were adequately paid for the jobs that they did. It is questionable that they were given a level playing field. The company likely would not rate as a high favorite as a company for which to work and spend a career.

What do you think was the problem?

What would you do if you were in Jack's position?

- Nothing?
- Would you go to the (new) higher management?
- Would you go to HR?
- Would you try to resolve issues with Donald?
- To whom would you report during the managers' fight?
- Should Eddie have simply accepted the lesser job?
- Would you look for another job?
- Other?

What would you do if you were in Eddie's position?

Were the other project team members treated fairly?

Case 9

AFFAIRS of the OFFICE:
The Boss' Trouble Maker

Key Players:

- Melvin: Manager, **Boss**
- Joseph: Senior Engineer
- Melly: Administrative Assistant to the Boss
- Jerry: Senior Engineer

Synopsis:

Joseph and Jerry were senior engineers working for a large corporation on Government contracts. They were two of about twenty researchers, mostly men, who had their own individual research projects. Joseph had reported to the manager, Melvin, for about two years, and Jerry somewhat longer. Melly was Melvin's administrative assistant. She was in her late twenties and considered by the men to be quite attractive and well dressed, perhaps a little on the provocative side. She was outstanding in some secretarial work, keeping good computer records and filings. Other things were not good. She was not well liked by many in the organization. She was discourteous to the engineers, almost abusive, spent time on the phone with personal calls, came in late and took long lunch breaks. However, the main complaint was that she limited the engineers' access to their boss. She intercepted his email and sometimes deleted it. Many, including Joseph and Jerry, strongly resented that and blamed the boss. They felt these actions impeded their progress, as from time to time they needed management decisions and guidance. If anyone said anything about her conduct, the boss would just laugh and shrug it off as nothing important.

Joseph was asked to perform the duties of the manager for a three-week period while the boss was to be away on a trip out of the country. Ordinarily Jerry, with more experience with the boss, would stand in for Melvin, but on this occasion he also had to spend some time away from the home office. Joseph moved into Melvin's office. On the first day, Joseph answered Melly's phone while she was away from her desk and it was her husband calling. When told about the call, Melly shushed Joseph and said, "Don't say that, no one knows I have a husband." Joseph thought that was strange, but didn't pursue it.

Joseph found that to do his own work as well as that of the boss, he had to work into the night. He was in the boss's office working alone one night when Melly popped into the office. She said, "I was shopping in the area and I saw your office lights on. I stopped to show you what I just bought." With that, she seductively raised her skirt and showed him her frilly underwear. When Joseph found his voice, he said, "Don't do that, someone else might be here and walk by in the hallway." She said, "OK, I'll close the door." This was the first of several similar night visits.

One day at quitting time, Melly whispered to Joseph that she wanted to talk to him, but she wanted to do it over drinks at a local pub. She suggested that they leave the office separately, to avoid drawing attention, and meet at her car in the parking lot. Joseph did her bidding. The next day, Joseph's friend Jerry called Joseph aside and told him there was something he should know. Melly had told Jerry to watch out the office window and he would see Joseph following her to the parking lot. "He stalks me", Jerry told Joseph she had said. Joseph started to explain, and Jerry stopped him and said, "I know what happened. She's setting you up. Be careful."

Later discussions between Joseph and Jerry concluded with the belief that Melvin, their boss, and Melly were having some kind of non-business relationship. She now wanted Joseph to become involved, and become under her control. Jerry had been through it all himself, but had resisted. Blackmail was not out of the question.

On Friday of the third week Joseph found a letter on his desk from Melly. It was a resignation, effective immediately. He was puzzled that this had come as a complete surprise. He talked to his friend Jerry who suggested he call the HR (Human Resources) office. The HR manager suggested they have a meeting and discuss the event. HR, along with the higher management, had decided to give Melly an alternative, be fired outright or accept a monetary offer to resign and slip out quietly. They felt that it should be done while Melvin was away.

Melvin's first job when he returned was to interview applicants for Melly's replacement. He and Joseph avoided any discussion of Melly.

What Went Right:

- The technical work ran fairly smoothly.
- Joseph succeeded in his three weeks of managerial duty.
- The higher management, along with HR, resolved the perceived problem without repercussions.

What Went Wrong:

- Employee communication with the boss was sidetracked.
- The boss was believed to have had an affair with his employee.
- It was strongly suspected that the employee had threatened to blackmail the boss.
- The effectiveness of the organizational unit suffered.
- Two (or more) families' relations were placed in jeopardy.
- HR was concerned about the possibility of a sexual harassment lawsuit against the company.

Lessons Learned:

- Sometimes things not seen from within are obvious to outsiders.
- Stop and don't allow questionable personal relationships between boss and subordinates.
- Be careful of predators of both genders. Harassment works both ways. While most think of harassment as the boss harassing the lower level employee, it can actually happen the other way around.
- The boss can be induced into a threat of blackmail.
- Things can go very badly if the relationship ends.
- Appearance means everything.

Outcome:

The organization recovered and survived without a scandal. Melly was terminated and was replaced. The boss again became an effective leader.

Assessment of Management:

This case has the elements of the so-called office affair where things can go wrong, and did start to go wrong. It involved a forbidden romantic relationship between a boss and his subordinate. All cautionary writings on the subject warn of what can go wrong, especially if the relationship ends.

Melvin, the boss had allowed himself to get into a compromising position that threatened his career and his marriage. He allowed himself to become susceptible to blackmail. It can't be predicted to what extent the problem might have grown if not stopped. Already, in effect, he was being blackmailed into giving Melly everything she wanted and allowing her to run his organization.

Fortunately HR and the higher management learned of the problem and made the decision to terminate Melly's employment. Melvin was responsible for allowing the situation to get out of hand. However, Melvin was of great value to the company and, quite simply, Melly was not. They cited the way she was treating the researchers as being intolerable. Melly had to go. The management had the problem of stopping a scandal before it became public knowledge. The affair could have made the newspapers and caused great embarrassment to the company. They offered her a substantial severance payoff and instructed her to resign. HR and the company attorney got her to sign a statement that she would not sue the company. She accepted, and the unit got back to normal operation. It seemed to be a good thing that Joseph served temporarily in the boss's position, and his friend Jerry perceived just what was going on.

What do you think was the problem?

What should Joseph have told Melvin on his return?

What would you do if you were in Joseph's position?

Do you think management and HR did the right thing?

- By firing Melly?
- By giving Melly an alternative to resign?
- By firing Melly while Melvin was away?
- What risk do you think the company took?
- Was Joseph at any kind of risk?

Case 10

CULTURE SHOCK:
East is East, West is West

Key Players:

- Troy: **Boss**
- Duane: Engineer, Individual Contributor

Synopsis:

The Company was preparing to enter a new evolutionary step in advanced microcircuit technology. A new wing to accommodate research and development in this new technology was built onto the west end of the existing research and development (R&D) facility. It was designated as the West Wing. However the new laboratory housed in the West Wing was soon being referred to as the Far East Wing by the existing staff. That type of work seemed to attract large numbers of engineers and scientists from Asia.

The R&D facility had traditionally been a melting pot of global engineers and scientists. The policy had always been to solicit the highest qualified people without regard to national origin. It was quite common to hear people speaking English with many accents, for example, Japanese, Chinese, Indian, Russian, Hungarian, Bolivian, etc. It seemed that the largest segment of the staff in the new laboratory were of Asian descent. This presented no problem, as all employees were given courses in cultural diversity, and the sciences were the same for communication purposes. Everyone was already familiar with and enjoyed the global relationships, for after all, it was a learning environment.

Troy, the manager selected to head the laboratory, was originally from the Peoples' Republic of China (PRC). Troy had grown up and done his undergraduate work in the PRC, and had received his engineering Ph.D. at a prestigious university in the United States. Troy was proficient in the English language. Duane was an engineer in the laboratory with over twenty years' experience. Duane and Troy got along well. They were both easy going, friendly and polite. They liked each other.

Troy had no established reporting procedures, and Duane assumed that Troy used the procedure of management by exception, that is, stay away if everything is going well. From time to time Duane would initiate a meeting to discuss specific subject matters, such as funding or getting managerial support. Troy usually went along with Duane's ideas.

Duane prepared and presented a meticulous Microsoft Power Point™ show on the concept of a new integrated circuit chip and requested a commitment for a certain amount of internal funding. After a question and answer period with Troy and other staff, Duane left with the understanding that he was to go ahead as planned, and just as he had presented. Sometime later he discovered that no funding had been approved. Another meeting with Troy left Duane confused. Troy acted as though the prior meeting had not taken place, so Duane opened his notebook and went through the points of agreement. Duane felt he was fortunate to have taken detailed notes.

The same scenario repeated itself at a series of later meetings. Duane felt that if the answer were "no", then Troy should have said "no", and he would have stopped wasting effort, or would have changed his strategy. Duane became angry about the way his manager had treated him. As time went on, Duane began to suspect there was something wrong between the cultural backgrounds of himself and Troy. He pretty well confirmed that from lunchtime conversations with his colleagues. He just didn't know what to do about it.

What Went Right:

- The technical aspects of the project went well.
- The manager was readily accessible.
- Language in the multi-culture was not a factor.

- The company provided training on implementation of diversity policies.
- The company hired the most competent technical people available.
- Duane eventually discovered the problem, and took steps to improve.

What Went Wrong:

- While language was not a problem, *communication* was definitely a problem.
- The project suffered because of the communication problem.
- Diversity training had not been effective for neither the manager nor the employee.
- Troy could not change his business culture, nor could Duane change his.
- The non-Chinese engineers had little or no concept of the Chinese business culture.

Lessons Learned:

- There are fundamental differences between the cultures of the East and West that affect people at all levels, and many relationships.
- The differences extended far deeper than what Duane experienced.
- Internal diversity can be good for a business if understood.
- Internal diversity can wreck a business if not understood.
- Cultural diversity in business must be resolved for success.
- The company's concentration on diversity had been primarily on the legal ramifications of discrimination, which was not sufficient.
- The usual diversity training only teaches people to get along amicably.
- Training should include the business thought processes as well as social differences.

■ An understanding of the reasons behind the great differences between the East and West cultures would be very helpful, for both East and West.

Outcome:

The program struggled along inefficiently. Conditions improved as Duane and Troy held further discussions and resolved individual issues.

Assessment of Management:

Duane did not know that Chinese people don't like to say "no". In Troy's culture a "no" is like an insult and causes "loss of face". Loss of face, in the Eastern culture, affects both participants. Friendly relationships are considered a priority over business.

Troy had been hired as manager for his expertise in the technical field. Neither the manager nor the employees were prepared to cross the great cultural divide between the thought processes of the East and West. People in these situations for the first time don't even realize that these cultural differences exist. Study of the Eastern culture goes back to the Tao and teachings of Confucius, whereas that of the West goes back to Socrates, Aristotle and Plato. The Easterner seeks harmony within the whole of the community, and the Westerner looks for individualism. The Easterner strives for reduction of conflict within the group, and the Westerner encourages debate. True to the Western business culture, the thought process for hiring was to place the best technically qualified individual in the leading role. The Eastern thought process for hiring would likely be based on personal relationships and trust.

Troy, in his Eastern culture, was striving for stability and harmony within the group, as within a family. The financial aspects were not primary concerns as in Duane's Western culture. Duane simply wanted "yes" and "no" answers. The manager did not think much of negotiations and contracts, but focused on trust and loyalty and previous relationships. Duane liked to spell everything out in detail, as if in a contract. He felt that based on negotiation, a contract -- though verbal and informal, did exist. It spelled out what each party was to do, when, where and for what in return. The consideration of fairness is determined by the negotiation, though it is not unusual to get together and renegotiate changes, as to be of benefit to both parties.

Duane thought their negotiations had failed, and rightfully so, since he would leave their meetings without a good understanding of what had transpired. The Eastern business philosophy is to become friends first, and then attend to business. That part of the relationship worked, though the opposite order is the custom in the West. The two got along well personally.

In the R&D environment, the "totem pole" concept of ranking company employees based on their importance to the company was used for personnel evaluation. Troy's culture has trouble determining one's performance because they all operate as a whole. But in Duane's culture, everyone is assigned individual tasks as negotiated and is evaluated based on his sole performance. Time is looked at differently, as the Eastern culture thinks of time in the process. The West considers time to be linear, with a deadline. Time is equated with money.

This whole subject of cultural business diversity is very complex and is subject to further study. While the East and West differences have been long recognized in the world of global trade, the trend of working together is rapidly growing at the local business levels. Duane, in his dealings with his boss, Troy, had just scratched the surface.

The resources below are recommended for further reading on the business cultural differences between the East and West. Duane, as well as others in the unit, should become more knowledgeable of the cultural differences. Of course, the Easterners should also, but it should be easier as they are living in the Western environment. At the same time, more Westerners are integrating into Eastern environments. That is the nature of global business that is now a pervading issue with companies such as Duane's.

The following list provides interesting reading about the distinctions.

1) Chen, Ming-Jer. *Inside Chinese Business: A Guide for Managers Worldwide,* Harvard Business School Press, Boston, MA. 2001. ISBN 1-57851-232-8.

2) Nisbett, Richard E. *The Geography of Thought: How Asians and Westerners Think Differently ... and Why,* Free Press, A Division of

Simon & Schuster, Inc., New York, NY. 2003. ISBN 0-7432-1646-6; ISBN 0-7432-5535-6(Pbk).

3) Seligman, Scott D. *Chinese Business Etiquette: A Guide to Protocol, Manners, and Culture in the People's Republic of China,* Time Warner Book Group, New York, NY. 1999. ISBN 0-446-67387-0.

4) Collins, Robert, MBA; and Block, Carson, Esq.: *Doing Business in China for Dummies,* Wiley Publishing Company, Hoboken, NJ. 2007. ISBN 978-0-470-04929-7.

What was the problem?

What would you do if you were in Duane's position?

- Nothing?
- Would you go to higher management?
- Would you go to HR?
- Would you discuss cultural differences with Troy?
- Would you study the Eastern business culture?
- Would you recommend the company provide a different kind of training?
- Would you look for another job?
- Other?

Case 11

MISS CONFIDENTIALITY:
The (Non) Confidential Survey

Key Players:

- Carolyn: **Boss**
- Betty: Mathematician/Computer Scientist
- Bruce: Computer Scientist, witness
- Gary: Computer Scientist, witness
- Herbert: Team member alleged to have stolen credit
- Susan: HR Representative

Synopsis:

Betty, a Mathematician/Computer Scientist, had worked with an IT (Information Technology) team on several projects, and was currently working on a team project in biomedical engineering. At this same time, Betty was experiencing family problems at home, and at work she claimed that another team member had stolen credit for her work on the project. She had confided this information to Bruce and Gary, two computer scientists who worked for the same manager, Carolyn, though not on the same team as Betty. They believed her story because they knew the alleged thief, Herbert. Though they had never worked with him, they were familiar with his reputation. They also knew it was likely true because Herbert was not trained as a computer scientist, had no computer science background, and was out of his field in IT.

The HR (Human Resources) office conducted a confidential job survey of all employees, including the IT employees. The questionnaire asked such questions, for statistical reasons, as gender, years of experience, field of study and highest level of education. Then the questionnaire zoomed in on work related areas, such as degree of satisfaction with company, job, salary, workplace, manager, and provided space for comments. Susan was the HR representative who conducted the survey.

A returned (confidential) questionnaire indicated this (unidentified) employee, who happened to be Betty, was dissatisfied with the company, her job, her work, her salary, and her manager. She complained that a fellow team member had stolen credit for her work. Comments indicated that she was so distraught she was thinking of suicide!

After Susan and her HR associates had evaluated the surveys, the IT Manager, Carolyn, went door to door up and down the hallway stopping at each door to ask the question, "Did you threaten suicide on the questionnaire?" The IT Manager would then follow up by saying, "Oh, I know it wasn't you, you aren't a woman Ph.D. mathematician working on" such and such, effectively identifying the person in question. No one other than Betty would fit this precise description. That was Carolyn's and HR's way of covering up the lack of confidentiality. They already knew who the respondent was. Now they had to decide what to do.

Bruce and Gary immediately figured out Carolyn's ploy. They got together and discussed the unethical way in which the incident was handled by their management. They didn't say anything to Betty. They just assumed Carolyn went to Betty's office, and probably got a confession. However, the worst was yet to come. A few days later Carolyn called Betty into her office and informed her that she was fired. Bruce and Gary learned of this action when Betty came to them seeking advice and moral support.

Betty had to go quickly and quietly. The company used a questionable, but not unheard of, tactic, that is, the management granted a sum of money to a local university to employ Betty on a special one-year research project.

Gary and Bruce kept in touch with Betty at her new job. She went through a period of depression, but eventually recovered. She resolved her problems at home, and when her year was over at the university she moved on to another company, and again worked with several of her former associates who had moved on also.

What Went Right:

- The story had a happy ending.
- The employee in this case did not do anything drastic.
- The actions exposed flaws in the survey system.
- The IT and HR management got answers from the employees.
- In a way, the survey may have prevented disastrous consequences.
- The survey provided information that could have been useful in improving the work environment, and correcting problems that existed. That was what the employees were expected to believe.

What Went Wrong:

- The claimed confidentiality of the survey failed, and was exposed.
- The IT and HR management got answers they didn't like.
- Instead of helping Betty, the company fired her.
- Carolyn allowed Herbert to continue, even though he was not a qualified contributor.
- The team with Betty dispersed, several left the company.
- Bruce and Gary leaked the full story to all members of the IT organization.
- The employees of the IT organization lost faith in their manager and HR.

Lessons Learned:

- "Confidential" surveys may not be confidential.
- It does not pay to rate one's manager in a "confidential" survey.
- Don't take domestic problems from home to work as Betty did.
- When someone acts unethically (eg., steals credit), don't work with that person again.

- Don't depend on management's help for emotional problems, though there are EAP's, (Employee Assistance Programs). The EAP's help the company in issues involving insurance and lawsuits.
- Employee Assistance Programs also are not as confidential as advertised.

Outcome:

The project was discontinued, the team dispersed, the employee fired. The managers lost credibility with the employees.

Assessment of Management:

There clearly was no confidentiality in the so-called "confidential job survey". Generally "confidential" surveys need to be read carefully. Sometimes the confidentially statement may mean effectively "that you can tell us, but we promise not to share your information with anyone else." Or it may mean that "your identity may be kept secret even from us, the surveyors." The latter is generally what is believed by the employees to be true for employee surveys. Many employees believe that they can fill out surveys, state their grievances honestly and even lower the boom on their managers, and that their identity will not be known, and therefore be immune to any retaliation.

Another misconception is that the HR (Human Resources) office acts as an independent third party and takes a neutral position in disputes between the employee and his/her functional management. HR may try to resolve differences, but make no mistake that HR works for the company. The HR management strives for the solution it perceives to provide the greatest benefit to the company. Of course, HR managers may be biased by their own integrity. In this case, since there were questions in the survey about the IT manager, the IT manager should not have been allowed to see the actual questionnaires received by HR.

In the instant case there was unethical collusion between IT Manager, Carolyn, and HR Rep, Susan. The IT team member, Betty, was identified and tied to the "confidential" job survey immediately.

The IT Manager made a thinly disguised effort of covering up the lack of confidentiality. In fact she went beyond that by disclosing the identity of the employee to others in the IT unit. She broke both of the confidentiality premises stated earlier. It is not known if the survey was intentionally designed to identify employee respondents, but it may have been. The lesson is that a respondent should use a great deal of caution.

The company, as do many companies, had an Employee Assistance Program (EAP) that provided confidential assistance to employees, covering many subjects that apply to the physical and mental health. Mental health includes such as alcohol or drug abuse and others. When this employee needed such assistance, it was not provided. Proper application of EAP services is intended to benefit the health of the employee and to help the company to defend lawsuits. It should be noted that under the laws of New York State (and similarly other states) that certain instances require reporting to law enforcement, for instance: child or elderly abuse, threats or acts of murder, suicide, or Government overthrow. It remains unknown if EAP would have helped. It might, but was not given a chance.

Confronted with the gravity of the "threat of suicide", whether serious or not, the managers had to take quick action. These managers didn't want blood on the floor or walls during their watch. They had to get rid of the threat.

Betty was called in by Carolyn, and with the backing of her management and HR, she fired Betty using the stated reason of "deteriorated performance". Considering Betty's state of mind, the performance appraisal was probably true. No report of the "threat of suicide" was ever reported to any outside authority, nor was EAP even consulted. They just passed the problem on to Betty's next employer. In Betty's state of mind, it is reasonable to assume that she would be unable to find another job on her own.

News spread quickly. It's unlikely that the instant case produced an out-of-character action by the IT Manager. This IT Manager, Carolyn, would never be trusted again, if she had ever been. Most likely the employees already knew the manager was not trustworthy, and should have acted accordingly. Actually, Betty in the instant case should have known, and it is likely that she cast her caution aside because of the personal problems confronting her.

It appeared to Bruce and Gary that the managers, including Carolyn's boss, were concerned about their own jobs and with no concern for the employee who desperately needed help. Bruce and Gary were disillusioned by the events that took place.

What should Betty have done differently?

Who was the bad guy here?

- Carolyn?
- Susan?
- Betty?

What would you do if you were in Bruce's or Gary's position?

- Nothing?
- Would it change your perception of the company, Carolyn or HR?
- Would you go to higher management?
- Would you go to the HR management?
- Would you try to help Betty?
- Would you look for another job?
- Do you think EAP (Employee Assistance Program) could have helped? EAP claims "confidentiality".
- Would you contact EAP on Betty's behalf?

What would you do if you were Carolyn's boss?

What responsibility did the company have for Betty?

Case 12

WHO'S THE BOSS:
The Two Boss Dilemma

Key Players:

- Sam: **Boss 1**
- Fred: **Boss 2,** reporting to Sam
- Neil: Engineer/Computer Scientist
- Stewart: Engineer/Computer Scientist

Synopsis:

Neil and Stewart, both trained in electrical engineering and computer science, worked in a research and development (R&D) environment. Both held MS degrees. They worked together on projects encompassing both engineering and computer science. They reported to a manager, Sam, who held a Ph.D. in computer science but was not very well qualified in engineering. As far as Neil and Stewart's projects were concerned, Sam generally followed their advice. They knew what they were doing on their projects and had a loose relationship with Sam. They didn't think he was a good manager, but they were reasonably satisfied with him in their limited relationships. They did the work they enjoyed, made contributions to the company's needs, and annually received at least what they considered fair salaries.

In a restructuring move the R&D center made some organization changes. Some organizations were eliminated and others combined. Sam picked up some extra people. Neil and Stewart had worked for Sam for about three years and were not concerned about Sam's management. Others in the unit didn't like reporting to Sam because they simply considered him to be overloaded. A decision was made to add a layer of program managers between Sam and functional groups, thereby reducing Sam's overload by splitting up those reporting directly. Neil and Stewart were put into a group with several other engineers and computer scientists and were to report to a man named Fred, who in turn reported to Sam.

Fred had a Ph.D. in physics, a fact later learned by Neil and Stewart. They had thought that Fred was a computer scientist. He was always seen in his office in front of a computer terminal. They had no idea what he was doing. They had very little interaction with Fred, and continued to interface with Sam as they had previously done. They felt that in actuality they had been demoted by having to report to Fred, a lower level manager.

They had submitted a request to Sam, which Sam turned over to Fred for resolution. Fred told Neil and Stewart that the request had been turned down by Sam. Fred told them they should have brought the request to him first, and it would have been approved. But now it was too late. Sam later said that not he, but Fred had turned down the request. This act confused Neil and Stewart.

Not only had Neil and Stewart circumvented Fred, but Sam circumvented Fred also by going directly to Neil and Stewart. Neil started to notice that often he received instructions from Sam, and later Fred would distort or even contradict what Sam had said. This got to the point such that Neil and Stewart would not believe anything that Fred said. Fred was considered totally untrustworthy.

It came time for Neil's annual job performance review. Neil filled out the customary computer documents describing his past year's activities and accomplishments, and his next year plan outlining his goals and objectives. He and Fred had a short meeting and discussion. They came to an amicable agreement.

Neil was appalled when he received Fred's response that went to Sam and to the HR office. It read something like, "Neil successfully completed his projects, but not everyone thinks the projects are important." And it went on to say, "I don't know enough about his work to make an evaluation." However, he did make an evaluation anyway, turning in a bad report. In all of Neil's years in engineering, he had never before received a bad performance rating. Since salary action was based on the annual performance evaluation, he expected little or none. He was quite angry.

What Went Right:

- The technical work ran fairly smoothly.

What Went Wrong:

- Fred was not trusted.
- Fred was not qualified.
- The department promoted the person with the highest college degree for PR purposes without regard to qualifications.
- Fred admitted he was not a competent manager.
- Fred lied to his subordinates.
- Neil was stuck with a bad performance appraisal in his HR records.

Lessons Learned:

- Don't assume a manager with a different technical background will remain passive and not cause trouble.
- The person with the highest level college degree may often be promoted for PR purposes without regard to qualifications.
- Keep a copy of everything agreed upon with your manager.
- A bad boss can devastate morale.
- A bad boss can negatively affect careers.

Outcome:

Confusion and anger resulted. No one knew to which boss he/she should report. Employees' careers were negatively affected.

Assessment of Management:

In the research and development center it was prestigious for all managers to hold PhD's. In Fred's case, the Ph.D. was in physics, a discipline that had no relationship to any work going on in Sam's area. Sam and his higher management felt that Fred's assignment would provide the prestige, and the job of managing professional people would be easy and unchallenging. After all, he could have turned down the job if he wanted, but there was really nothing going on at the center in his field of study. This was unfortunate for those who had to report to such a manager. Perhaps it was unfortunate for Fred also to be working outside of his field.

While the company in general had many technical managers with MBA degrees in the business departments, this was not the case for the R&D center. Technical managers typically held Ph.D. degrees in their technical specialties, and non technical managers, such as HR, had Ph.D.'s. in their fields. These were for status and PR, not for practical purposes. Fred was a misfit cast into the wrong job. Many managers were thrust into management roles after they had become obsolete in their technical fields. In this case, Sam and Fred were acting as co-managers, which was against the company procedures. This is as it should be. Such arrangements seldom work.

In the majority of cases such as this the only formal training managers received was going to seminars usually conducted by professors or training companies. These training sessions were often conducted at resorts with golf courses where the managers would convene away from the daily activities and interruptions at the workplace. Many considered it an off site fun activity for managers. It was a bonus for being managers.

What would you do if you were in Neil's position?

- Nothing?
- Would you try to resolve issues with Fred?
- Would you try to resolve issues with Sam?
- Would you request a meeting with both together?
- Would you go to HR?
- Would you go to higher management?
- Would you look for another job?
- Other?

Robert M. Hardy

What would you do if you were in Stewart's position – having knowledge of Neil's performance appraisal?

Case 13

AGE DISCRIMINATION:
The Case Couldn't Lose

Key Players:

- Henry: **Boss**
- Carl: Laid off Employee, one of many
- Mike: Head Layoff Specialist
- HR: HR Representative
- Hatchet Lady: HR Rep in charge of layoff
- Carl's Attorney
- Company's Attorney
- Outsourced Layoff Specialists
- Raymond: An older company retiree

Synopsis:

Carl was a fifty eight year old engineer just short of his thirtieth anniversary with the company. He reported to Henry, a research and development manager with a computer science background, who was considered marginally competent by his subordinates. Henry, though, at age forty, considered himself upwardly mobile and stayed attuned to the wishes of company headquarters. Henry had been a manager in the same position for about four years, the longest time he had spent at any one of four previous companies.

Carl had a long background of significant accomplishments, was paid a competitive salary, and was only two years away from the earliest retirement age of sixty. He was the oldest of about twenty employees under Henry's command.

Carl had become aware of Henry's bias against age at a salary adjustment time, when Henry came into Carl's office and announced that he had "good news and bad news". Carl would be getting a lump sum payment, but would not get a salary increase. (Companies sometimes give lump sums instead of salary increases during tough economic times.) However, Henry told Carl he was "at the wrong place on the age curve". Such curves were published annually by professional organizations, for example, the IEEE (International Electrical and Electronics Engineers) Society. These charts are made from member survey responses and are not intended for salary determination. The charts do, however, show that engineers' salaries peak at about the age of fifty-to-fifty five, a typical bell shaped curve. Those younger and those older make less money. Carl's age put him beyond the salary peak, which showed him to be paid higher than the curve. Carl had been aware of such charts, but had no idea they were being used for salary determination. Carl responded, "Henry, that is age discrimination and it's illegal!" Henry shrugged it off and mumbled something like, "It's not really an age curve, but some curve that HR uses."

After that incident, Carl started paying attention to Henry's behavior and statements he made about older people. They were frequent and witnessed by numerous others. It became clear that Henry was obsessed about age. Two years passed and at each salary action time (once a year) Henry gave Carl a lump sum payment. The problem with lump sums is that the salary level remains the same and does not increase equity in the company's pension plan. After the third year, Henry gave Carl a reasonable salary increase based on a percentage of base salary.

Then the research and development department decided to lay off as many as ten percent of its total workers. Henry was given a quota for layoff. It seemed natural that Henry would select Carl.

Corporate headquarters sent an HR (Human Resources) representative to assist in the task. She was given the unaffectionate designation as the "Hatchet Lady". Under her direction, HR contracted with an outside company specializing in all aspects of layoffs. The leader of the layoff team of specialists was a person named Mike. The duties of Mike and the layoff specialists were basically twofold:

1. To plan the coming layoff and prepare the company such that the company would avoid, or at least win, any resulting lawsuits; and

2. To set up an outplacement center to assist in writing resumes, providing communications and clerical services, and office space for contacting and interviewing prospective employers. This off-site service would separate the laid off workers from those retained, to avoid morale problems.

Under Mike's layoff specialists' guidance, HR set about the task of reviewing and changing operating procedures relative to layoff. Since the beginning of Carl's long employment there had been a procedure that provided the award of one week's pay for each year of employment in a lack of work situation. In this case, before the layoff, the HR office rewrote the layoff benefits procedure to eliminate this provision for employees such as Carl. Carl qualified for early retirement in a layoff situation, in accordance with another procedure. Unchanged, this rewritten procedure would have amounted to a significant amount of money for Carl. This represented one of several procedure changes to save the company a lot of money at the expense of the laid off employees.

Carl had seen layoffs before, but they had always been related to business conditions and were understood by the employees. He had also seen employee dismissals related to performance evaluations. Carl's performance appraisals had always been excellent throughout his career. If age discrimination was not clear, Carl's management had made it quite clear, when Henry told Carl that his salary was "too high for his age". In other words, Carl's salary should be lower in comparison with that of younger people. Henry would later lie about this statement, even though witnessed by another employee.

Before layoff announcement, Mike and his team of hired layoff experts held training sessions for the department's managers. Managers, including Henry, were taught what day of the week the laid off workers should be notified, and what those selected for layoff should be told about why each was selected. They had a list of frequently asked questions (FAQ), with answers prepared in advance. They even had another word for layoff, or downsizing. It was now known as "rightsizing".

Mike meticulously laid out a plan for Henry and the other managers.

1). Tuesday is the "right" day to notify the employees selected for termination.
2). Don't do it on Monday, but allow the employees to get settled into their week's work. People sometimes take a long weekend and are absent on Mondays, or slow getting restarted.
3). Don't do it just before the weekend, like Thursday or Friday. That is to avoid giving the weekend to allow anger to grow.
4). With notification on Tuesday, then Wednesday is the day reserved for HR to explain the company benefits available to those who were being laid off.
5). The contracted layoff expert staff (Mike's staff) would then give seminars to the laid off workers on Thursday and Friday to coach the workers on how to resolve their anger and start concentrating on finding new jobs outside the company. The off-site facility for the laid-off employees was open.

When Henry told Carl that he had been selected for layoff he knew age was the reason. After a short time other laid off employees began to talk to each other. It became apparent within a few days that age was the main determining factor in all the layoff selections. A little research showed that all employees selected for layoff were of the oldest age group in their respective work units.

The immediate response was for the laid off workers to scramble for new employment opportunities. The older employees found great difficulty in finding new jobs. The economy in general was not in good shape. Companies that were hiring were looking for younger employees at lower salaries for their long term potential. Time dragged on and days became weeks, and weeks became months. There was talk about lawsuits.

The result was that lawsuits were contemplated. Carl joined those talking to lawyers about bringing a lawsuit based on age discrimination. The word was out. Several lawyers contacted Carl about handling his case. In the group, Carl had a longtime friend who was an attorney. Though he was apprehensive, he felt he couldn't turn down his friend. Lawyers were hungry. Suits were filed with the State Court.

The company had already hired an outside law firm, with attorneys commonly referred to as tricksters who were reputed to ask unrelated questions and would try to distort anything favorable to the laid-off employee. The company's hired lawyers came across as grossly incompetent and decidedly dishonest, but fiercely determined. These lawyers acknowledged that the company's managers were incompetent, but that was not against any law.

Examinations Before Trial (EBT) were scheduled. (EBT is customary to allow attorneys to interview witnesses for both sides before going to trial. EBT records are used for submittal to the court for the hope of a summary judgment avoiding a trial.) Before the EBT Carl had requested a copy of his personnel records. HR could not find appraisal records. However, the company's lawyer "found" the records. At EBT, the company's lawyer handed Carl a "good" appraisal document and a (modified) "bad" appraisal document (accidentally) stuck together. He revealed that HR used a "*Salary vs. Age Curve*", with age camouflaged as "*Years-since-BS degree*" to determine salary -- clear evidence of age discrimination. The company's lawyer tried to show on the record for the judges that salary determination according to years since anything except birth had nothing to do with age, since "age" was not written on the graph. They contended the fact that only older workers were selected was purely coincidental.

The company lawyer used tactics in Carl's EBT that should be remembered by any laid off employee facing EBT. In the EBT he made statements to the record, rather than asking questions. Many statements made by the lawyer were not true, but not being phrased as questions did not get answers. Many times he would preface a question with the phrase, "Would it surprise you if ...?" From such a phrase, one reading the transcript might infer that the lawyer's preface was a true statement, when, in fact, it was totally false. One of the witnesses questioned had the perfect answer every time he was asked a question with that phrase, "Would it surprise you if ...?" The witness' answer was, "No. Nothing the managers did would surprise me. I just can't predict what they might do." The company lawyer also strayed from facts to hypotheses. He asked questions about statistics, revealing that he had not had Statistics 101. He asked what he thought were engineering questions, but had no relevance. But, then, how would a judge know it was not relevant?

Another EBT example involved licensed professional engineers, such as Carl, who were required by state law to annually complete continuing educational courses (referred to as CEU's, Continuing Education Units). The company lawyer wanted the record to convince the reviewing judges (or juries) that Carl "must not be qualified if he had to keep improving his education". (One might think that lawyers would have the same requirements).

The case progressed in such a direction that Carl could not lose.

The company lawyer petitioned the court for a summary judgment. This meant that a judge would review the case (the EBT transcripts) and determine if there was sufficient evidence to go forward with a jury trial. The company hoped that the judge would reject the case based on lack of merit, or more likely confusion in the EBT transcripts. The judge surprised and angered the company lawyer by ruling in Carl's favor.

The company's legal representative then appealed to the next higher court, the State Appellate Court and the higher court agreed to review the case. Carl and his attorney were well pleased and looked forward to the next step.

One day during the next several weeks of waiting for the appeal, Carl received a phone call out of the blue. It was from a company retiree named Raymond in Florida. Carl had known Raymond years before but had not known what had become of him, nor the circumstances of his retirement. Raymond still had connections within the company and had heard about the layoff and the court actions. He had some advice for Carl.

Raymond explained that he had retired about ten years earlier under similar circumstances. He had sued for age discrimination, won at the first court level and then lost on the company's appeal. He advised Carl that if the company offered a settlement, he should consider it carefully -- the first offer would be the best. He cautioned Carl, and his exact words were, that the company "had the State Appellate Court in its pocket." He repeated that phrase several times. The State Appellate Court and State Court of Appeals (highest state court) were made up of what are commonly called activist judges. As Raymond predicted, the company offered a small settlement, but Carl turned it down. After all, the evidence was overwhelming.

But, even so -- the company won at the second level. The State Appellate Court wrote the decision that speculated on what might have happened -- without regard to evidence. The court *speculated* that there "*may have been animus*" between Carl and his manager, Henry. In many states (including this state) the employee works "*at the pleasure of the employer*". That means that "*animus*" is a cause for dismissal. The court made up the "*animus*" issue, even though neither the employer nor the employee had brought up or even alluded to "*animus*" as an issue.

Carl and his lawyer had to re-read the court's decision, as they were concerned that the court had become confused and had decided on someone else's case. Since the same happened in the cases of the other employees, they concluded that they had faced a prejudiced court.

Carl's lawyer quickly filed an appeal to the highest court of the state. The State Court of Appeals would not look at the case. The judges turned it down without comment. The case, that could not lose, lost. Anger shifted from the bosses to the courts.

What Went Right:

- Evidence against the company was overwhelming.
- The State's lower court judge ruled on the side of Carl, the employee, as expected.
- The same happened for other layoff victims with separate lawsuits, and those with group lawsuits.
- AARP (American Association of Retired Persons) agreed to assist in the court cases. (Unfortunately, AARP was not brought into the act until appeals processes had started.)

What Went Wrong:

- Carl and others waited too long to sue in Federal Court. The time limit is 300 days.
- Henry, Carl's boss, lied in the EBT, Examination Before Trial.
- The company appealed with success the lower court judge's ruling, without any point of law.
- The State Appellate Court overturned the judge's ruling, citing bad judgment on the part of the lower court judge, not error of law.

- The State Appellate Court *speculated* on what might have happened, without regard to evidence of what really happened. The Court's written opinion stated that "there *may have been* animus", a totally made up issue by the State Appellate Court.
- The Court of Appeals, the state's highest court, rejected Carl's appeal of the Appellate Court's decision without comment.
- Carl was prevented from having his case tried by jury in a court of law.
- AARP was brought into the case too late.
- The same treatment was administered to the other cases.
- **The case, that could not lose, lost.**

Lessons Learned:

- Become familiar with the rules of the EEOC (Equal Employment Opportunity Commission) by the time you reach the age of discrimination (40).
- The company will try all means to prevent a jury trial.
- The company will likely make an offer based on their legal defense fees. If they do, the first offer will be the best offer. This is a strategy, so consider it carefully.
- Company's hired lawyers are hired to win. They will mislead any way they can to win. This is particularly true when involving employees in technical fields in which neither the lawyers nor the judges are competent.
- There is typically an examination before trial (EBT). Attorneys representing both sides interrogate witnesses from both sides. A court stenographer records the EBT.
- In the EBT, have your attorney question you to clarify misleading statements connected with ambiguous or non-relevant questions asked by the company's attorney. This is necessary for the record, and will make it more difficult for a judge to throw out the case. Otherwise it is just based on obtuse questions and misleading statements by the company's defense lawyers. The company lawyers are not expert in your field, and obtuse questions should be exposed to show irrelevance, incompetence, and deliberate intent to mislead.

- Be careful in answering hypothetical questions. Answer questions about facts. Beware of giving yes or no answers when it is clear that the company attorney has no idea what he is talking about. Remember he is not qualified in your profession.
- Be careful in answering questions prefaced with the phrase, "Would it surprise you if …?" There may be a tendency for one reading the EBT transcript to erroneously infer truth in the lawyer's preface.
- Remember that the company's lawyer has the objective of getting you to make misstatements on the record.
- Don't assume a state court will be fair.
- There is a big difference between ethics and law.
- It is not unlawful for company's management to be incompetent. It is not unlawful to be unfair in personnel performance evaluation.
- HR records belong to the company. It is not unlawful to change HR records without the employee's knowledge. Even though, as in this case, it may involve tampering with evidence.
- Expect activist judges. The state, in this case, had activist judges at the higher court levels.
- It is unlikely that a large company will lose on age discrimination in state courts where there are politically motivated judges. In this case, emphasis was placed on the political objective of retaining big companies within the state.
- Know the politics relating big companies with State Government.
- Judicial corruption is worldwide – "widespread bribery of judges around the world and inappropriate political interference in legal systems are denying millions their rights to a fair and impartial trial", a leading global anti-corruption group said.
- Very little else matters if the court is corrupt.
- Records show that such a lawsuit has a better chance in Federal Court. A lawsuit can be filed in Federal Court, but only within a 300-day time limit.
- It is generally better to sue in a Group Action (not the same as Class Action) than go alone. A pattern can be shown.
- AARP (American Association of Retired Persons) will assist in age discrimination cases. Always ask.

- Use an attorney experienced in labor lawsuits with a winning record. Fee must be based on contingency. (New York State's Bar Association is considering the issue of allowing attorneys to advertise as specialists, such as has not before been allowed. Attorneys currently say they "focus" on specialized areas. Under the new proposal they would be tested and certified in their specialty, for example, such as doctors. Other states are likely to follow.) Choose your attorney for his/her expertise and record in labor law.

- Do not assume your case will go to a jury trial. The company's attorneys will use all tactics they can to prevent a jury trial. That is why they want to be in control of the transcript of the EBT. Without a jury trial, the EBT transcript is the only written record for judgment.

- Juries can be assumed to be fair. A jury trial is not automatic.

- Your attorney may advise you to answer questions with "yes" and "no", and may tell you to not explain anything or give any information not specifically requested. The theory is to surprise the opposition in court with a jury. This is not necessarily good advice, since the case may not get to a jury. A judge may make judgment based on the contents of the EBT transcript. There are many instances where an explanation is necessary to cast truth in your favor.

- Remember that while the outsourced layoff specialists (Mike and his team) give the impression to be there to assist you in getting over the layoff trauma and finding another job, their allegiance is to the company that pays for their services, not you.

- Be prepared for a lengthy process, maybe several years. Memories will fade. Witnesses will disperse.

- Keep a good notebook.

- Nothing in a court of law is certain.

Outcome:

The plaintiffs (Carl and the other laid off employees) lost in State Courts. This was consistent throughout the company. On the other hand, other laid off employees who sued in Federal Court won their cases.

Assessment of Management:

A corporate wide layoff started about the time the Chairman and CEO was interviewed on national television and was asked what he would like to leave on his retirement. He stated that he would like to see a "young company". He had been chairman and CEO for many years, and was highly admired and respected by leaders of other companies. Under his guidance the company had prospered and the stock market value had multiplied. He was a model for other big corporations. He was now approaching his own retirement and wanted to go out with the company at its peak financial condition.

While the CEO was widely respected by the big business community, he was not well liked by the employees, and was feared by the company's management. CEO's are beginning to be scrutinized by the media, and some even go to jail for financial fraud. Business philosophy is changing from a hundred percent concentration on the bottom line, to more political focus on employee benefits, environment and the good of the community. The CEO sensed that it was time for him to get out, and it's been said he wanted to retire as a billionaire. The big company wide layoff was his last effort to increase the value of the stock.

The CEO had made it clear that the company owed no loyalty to the employee, as in a statement that the company offered a "level playing field for the employee to put in an honest week's work", and that "we are even every Friday", meaning that the employee was paid for his work, no more, no less, no loyalty.

It is well for employees to understand the management culture from the CEO on down to the lowest level. Orders may be given at the top level of management that cause otherwise honest managers in the chain to become dishonest, and even breakers of the law, to save their own jobs. In Carl's case, during his many years in the company, he had seen several CEO's come and go without any affect on his work and personal professional growth. By this time, Carl was beyond the point of making a career change to another company. He had to be prepared for retirement, but was not ready.

Carl had over his career worked for several different components of the company. His current job, working in the research and development component, had been the longest in duration. The research and development center traditionally received some of its funding from the business departments, as was assessed against their profits. The rest of its funding came from contracts to do specific R&D for various business departments, and a third source from contracts with the U.S. Government. Currently there were no R&D funding problems that would warrant a layoff. However, the business departments being assessed for R&D funding were having layoffs, supposedly for business and economic reasons. So the research and development department did what some called a "sympathy layoff". Business department managers saw some logic in this move.

Carl might have picked up a subtle clue when he was given a salary increase instead of a lump sum after having received lump sums for the previous three years. Within a few months after the salary adjustment, he was notified of his layoff. This resulted in his being able to receive only part of the salary increase. The company saved money by not giving a lump-sum payment when the employee would be selected for layoff. In a big company with many such employees, the savings are significant.

When the lawsuit started, Henry and HR panicked and started falsifying papers. For people like Carl, with many years of excellent and outstanding performance records, they manufactured fraudulent documents. They altered good appraisal documents with lead in text such as, "Carl's performance has been deteriorating for some time and is now unacceptable", with back dates. These documents were immediately suspected as fraud. Some employees, as Carl, had maintained good records that refuted the managers' false documents.

Carl's manager, Henry, had done things to protect himself, as well as had HR, things that they might not normally have done. One should always remember that they work for the corporation. HR works for the corporation and is not necessarily the employee's friend. Henry had aspirations of moving upward in the company. A cover-up was under way.

The fact was well known that Henry held a bias against older employees. This is true in many cases where younger managers are placed in charge of older employees. The plain truth is that they fear the more experienced workers, and one way to deal with this fear is with termination. And, of course, it is true in some situations that the older employees have become technically obsolete. However, that would be the exception in the R&D environment where engineers and scientists are continually advancing the state of the art. Carl had spent a career in developing new technology, and in some areas was the best of the best.

The company's lawyer defending against Carl's case was somewhat of a buffoon. Within his bumbling, he revealed that Carl's performance evaluation papers maintained by HR had been falsified by Henry, and with HR's concurrence. Carl independently confirmed his contention that Henry had falsified his personnel records. Carl contacted a friend within the department who was an expert computer programmer who hacked into Henry's computer to find and trace the suspicious documents. The computer documents showed the modification was date-time-stamped several months after the beginning of the lawsuit. Carl's lawyer, however, advised that this evidence could not be used as it was illegally gained information. As it turned out, the judges didn't care anyway.

Carl and his lawyer were confused that the company would be represented legally by such apparent incompetence. In looking back, it appeared that the company went through a routine, having had confidence that it would be taken care of by the courts, which is what happened.

The outsourced layoff specialist company's allegiance was to the company. Mike's team spent much rhetoric in trying to be convincing in the theory that they were there to help the laid off employees. The company wanted to outwardly appear to be benevolent to its employees. Most of the layoff victims were aware of the layoff specialty firm's role in the entire layoff process, and held the firm in low regard.

Carl and the other employees certainly made their own mistakes after the layoff. They should not have been taken by surprise by the layoff, or that older employees were targeted. Carl had known for some time that Henry was biased against older workers. As one witness, a retired manager, testified in the EBT, "One would have to be brain dead to not know that age discrimination was widely practiced within the company."

Further, they were not aware of the EEOC's (Equal Employment Opportunity Commission) Federal law that required age related law suits to be filed with the Federal Courts within three hundred days of the layoff event. They all ended up in the state courts already known to favor the big corporation. The word on the street was that "the company had the state judges in its pocket".

The judge for the lower court read carefully the court documents and made a decision in Carl's favor. Unfortunately the decision was overturned. The reason given was based on speculation, not fact. Carl and his attorney believed there was judicial corruption.

Judicial corruption appears to be a worldwide phenomena. Widespread bribery of judges around the world and inappropriate political interference in legal systems are denying millions their rights to fair and impartial trials. One only needs to go to the Internet or newspapers to find numerous references to corruption in the courts. A quick starting resource for information is: www.jail4judges.org, a watchdog organization dedicated to exposing and ousting crooked judges. *Transparency International* is a global coalition against corruption that provides worldwide statistics. It's generally recognized that there is little or no accountability except when occasionally one gets caught in the act of such as taking bribes. A famous case involved Richard "Dickie" Scruggs (www.law.com, June 2008) of Mississippi, the legendary tobacco trial lawyer who made Big Business tremble every time he set foot in court, pleaded guilty to conspiring to bribe a judge -- a case that sent him to prison and will spell the end of his storied legal career.

Another interesting case of judicial corruption occurred in Pennsylvania where two judges allegedly accepted over two million dollars from private juvenile detention centers to send youthful accused offenders to the centers. One of the (former) judges who pleaded guilty sought dismissal of a law suit filed on behalf of hundreds of children who claimed that he violated their civil rights by taking money for sending them to private detention centers. Former Luzerne County, Pennsylvania, Judge contended that he was entitled to "judicial immunity even if his decisions were corrupt."

In Carl's case the company appealed the judge's decision and the State Appellate Court overruled the decision. There was no point of law mentioned. The Appellate Court wrote that the judge had erred in judgment. The court wrote, "There was no evidence of age discrimination", and that "there may have been animus between Carl and his manager". That latter statement was a concept made up by the judges, and was not mentioned anywhere in any of the court records by the company or the employee. It served the high court's purpose in giving a reason for layoff.

It seems unlikely that a large company will lose on age discrimination in state courts where there are politically motivated judges. In this case, emphasis appeared to be placed on the political objective of retaining big companies within the state. Even the local newspaper printed a story about Carl's case titled, "The Same Old Story". It was happening all around in state courts. Such actions are more prevalent during bad economic times. It might have worked out differently in better economic times. But if the economy had been better the layoffs might not have taken place.

The company's legal team had the single purpose of winning. This should always be remembered. The company doesn't care how it is done, as long as the case is won! Fairness or justice is not a factor. Carl made his decision to seek legal action partly because of the actions of other victims of the layoff. He had enough evidence he could not possibly lose.

Carl made a major mistake of entering into a legal action with the counsel of an attorney who was a personal friend. Unfortunately his attorney was not experienced in labor law, misled Carl in many instances and caused the ending of a long time friendship. Carl's lawyer should have anticipated that the company would ask for a summary judgment, which it did. Even though Carl won in the first round before an honest judge, the company appealed to the State Appellate Court and Carl lost. Since the judges saw only the transcript of the EBT (assuming they might actually have read it), it was imperative that Carl's lawyer should have taken his opportunity to question Carl and set the EBT record straight where the company's lawyer had misled and confused the record. Carl's lawyer, knowing that Carl had such a "smoking gun" case, assumed that the company would offer a payoff, and he would reap a sizeable share of the award without doing anything. The company did offer a small payoff that Carl rejected. Carl's mistakes can't be over emphasized. This case should be remembered by others facing similar circumstances.

It is understandable that anger shifted from the bad managers who violated the law to the judges who let them get by with it.

There were no records of jury awards in the state courts, as no lawsuit ever reached a jury. The company was judged liable in similar cases in Federal Court with wide ranges of settlements.

One last point of advice in an age discrimination case is to remember that the statute of limitations on getting a suit into Federal Court is 300 days. Unfortunately Carl didn't know that. Carl, as well as others, busied himself with the hope and effort to find another job.

What would you do if you were in Carl's position?

- Nothing?
- Take early retirement?
- Try to negotiate a settlement?
- Contact the EEOC (Equal Employment Opportunities Commission)?
- Contact AARP (American Association for Retired Persons)?
- Replace your attorney?
- Join a group for a Group Action Lawsuit?
- Join a legal watchdog organization?
- Other?

How would you characterize the managers in this case?

What should Carl have done about his lawyer? Should he report him to the state bar association?

Do you think the falsified performance evaluation affected Carl's ability to find another job?

Should this have been a factor in the lawsuit?

Let's assume a reasonable person would see that the ruling was in conflict with the EBT transcript and the documents in evidence. So what could and should Carl have done about his loss with the Appellate Court?

In what ways could you do better in court? Is it possible?

Case 14

HE'S UP, HE'S DOWN, HE'S UNWOUND:
The Bi-Polar Boss

Key Players:

- John: The **Boss**
- Ellis: Engineer
- Larry: Engineer
- Adam: John's Boss

Synopsis:

The engineering team led by Ellis and Larry had invented and developed a new concept in industrial motor controls, the kind used primarily in factory production processes. Traditional technology had used mostly electro-magnetic devices to measure time and electrical current. The new technology would use embedded programmable microprocessor chips set up to prolong the life of motors and to protect the electrical wiring in the plant. The new motor control design concept had gained wide popularity within the company, which made and sold motors and motor controls, as well as being a big user of motors. Ellis and Larry reported to Program Manager, John, who had recently been assigned his first management job. John had previously worked with Larry and Ellis, and they both supported his promotion. John held a Ph.D. in electrical engineering and had a number of years of design experience in power systems and control systems.

A meeting was to be held in one of the corporation's several business headquarters in another state. Ellis and Larry were to present their model, and other departments within the company were to present their innovations, concepts and needs. The objective was to agree on a single design that would serve all applications company wide. Company department representatives came from U.S., Canada and Europe. At the last minute Larry, who was the recognized foremost motor expert, had to cancel out for personal reasons. It was too late to cancel and reschedule the meeting. They advised the Program Manager, John. John decided to attend in order to have two representatives at the meeting. The team thought it was a good idea, as he would have a chance to learn the project, and to meet the other interested parties.

Development team member, Ellis, had barely started his presentation when his program manager, John, jumped up to re-explain one of his slides, using such expressions as, "This is what Ellis is trying to say." He continued to do this, slide by slide, causing the presentation to exceed the allotted time. It was not over with Ellis' presentation. As each of the other scheduled speakers tried to make his presentation, the scene was repeated. John obviously intended to show that Ellis's concept was superior, and any other concept was flawed.

Chaos ensued. The meeting turned into disarray. All were confused. The meeting was adjourned without any decisions for follow on development. Ellis took the news back home and discussed the happenings with Larry and other team members. They decided to talk privately with John's manager, Adam. Adam listened sympathetically but didn't promise anything.

Adam did, however, talk to John. The next day John called a meeting of the team members. John had now gone from being overly enthusiastic about the project, to admonishing Ellis and cautioning the team against any further criticism of his management. John refused to accept any responsibility for the flop. He started making accusations that Ellis and Larry were not providing him with full details about the project. He accused them of trying to cut him out of the project. He went even further and accused Ellis of trying to get him fired by going over his head and complaining to Adam.

Larry, being the motor expert, later traveled to the other departments, including one in Europe in hopes of resurrecting the project. It was of no avail. The project was discontinued.

An attempt was made to recover and start another project. Ellis and Larry, as well as other team members, found John to appear to have mood swings from very enthusiastic about a project, and then at the first sign of a difficulty, to rant and rave. He told Adam and the upper management how great the project was going to be. He was just as quick to place blame and cause embarrassment to the team members whenever things went wrong. This put everyone under extreme stress. They all knew they faced a rough road ahead.

What Went Right:

- The team designed a good technical concept.
- The team brought several company components to work together effectively.
- The Program Manager, John, was ecstatic about the acceptance of the new design.

What Went Wrong:

- The program manager suddenly became an interference.
- The project was discontinued. It was not feasible to attempt recovery as it was too difficult to bring these participants, who were geographically separated, together again.
- John changed from applauding Ellis's and Larry's work to severely criticizing both them and their work.
- John refused to accept any responsibility for the failed project.
- Introduction of a new similar product to the market was delayed for several years.
- Higher management would not interfere with the tiff between the program manager and the team. Actually, Adam's involvement made things get worse.

Lessons Learned:

- An over zealous program manager can ruin a project.
- Project teams should thoroughly brief a new manager.
- Roles should be discussed and understood before any major event.

- Don't depend on general management to replace a bad manager they had picked.
- Erratic behavior such as displayed by John may result from a medical problem.

Outcome:

The project failed. The affiliations of the departments were disbanded. An opportunity was lost. The future of this team under the same management looked dismal.

Management Assessment:

John started as an ardent supporter of the project. John apparently thought he was helping Ellis to get his points across, when in fact he was causing Ellis great embarrassment, as well as putting the entire project in jeopardy. After that, the higher management (Adam) did nothing to resolve the situation, and the entire project failed. The episode caused great mistrust of the new program manager, casting doubt on any new projects with the same management.

Ellis and Larry, as well as other team members, witnessed John as he changed personalities when he was promoted from a team contributor to the boss of the team. Instead of being the calm participant, he had become in the eyes of the team, a tyrant.

John may have not been a good choice as manager in the beginning. This was his first job in a management role. A set of criteria should be reviewed for a prospective manager to qualify. No one can tell exactly how a new manager will act in certain circumstances. It appears that he was nervous and became overly emotional. On the other hand, he may have been a micro manager, and/or he may have thought he could be more effective in presentations than his subordinates. By the time that one gets to be a program manager in charge of engineers and technical projects, the technique of making presentations should have been mastered.

It is entirely possible that John might have a medical problem that caused him to exhibit bipolar behavior. He clearly showed highs and lows in his actions. The screening process for managers may not detect such a disorder, because questions about mental illness are not permitted in job interviews. That is, it is not permissible for the interviewer to bring up the subject. In this instance the promotion was from within, and likely no competitive interview ever took place. Since higher management took a passive role in the matter, Ellis and Larry might try giving John another chance, and try to keep him more involved in the next project.

Much has been written on the subject of bipolar behavior. People are now beginning to come out of the closet. Famous people are admitting to suffering from depression. However it is definitely a stigma in the work place. It is an illness sometimes referred to as manic-depressive, because the two extremes are alternately exhibited. Much writing has been directed to the person exhibiting the disorder. Other writings are directed to people who live with one with a bipolar disorder. Amazon.com offers many books on the subject, including:

Candida Fink, MD, and Joe Kraynak. *Bipolar Disorder for Dummies*, Wiley Publishing, Inc., Hoboken, NJ. 2007. ISBN-0-7645-8451-0.

In the February, 1998, issue of *Electrical Apparatus Magazine*, Richard B. Elsberry wrote "Bipolar disorder: Why are they calling it the CEO's disease?" in part," He's up! He's down! What is it with the boss? A new look at manic depression. One day your boss exhibits boundless energy, the next, total lethargy. At times his behavior is wild, impulsive, chaotic, creative. But he can as easily become withdrawn, suicidal, hopelessly depressed."

It could be indeed a very serious matter. In this case, it may have been well for the individuals that the project ended. It is unlikely that Ellis or Larry would be able to alleviate the problem with John. Higher management and the HR office also might be hindered by the law that prohibits asking questions about mental illness in job interviews. However, they are free to make employment decisions based on job performance. It is doubtful that John could ever be an effective manager.

What do you think was the problem?

What would you do if you were in Ellis's or Larry's position?

- Nothing?
- Do you think the management/employee relationship could ever work with John?
- Would you go to higher management?
- What should higher management do?
- Would you go to HR?
- Would you try to resolve issues with John?
- Would you look for another job?
- What would you do if John repeats his act at another presentation?
- What would you do if you believed John had a mood problem and needed medical attention?

Case 15

STOLEN CREDIT:
The Technology Thief

Key Players:

- Manager of Engineering: Second Boss
- Manager of Marketing and Planning: First Boss
- Harold: Last **Boss**
- Philippe: Design Engineer, project team leader
- Thomas: Systems Engineer
- Valerie: Software Designer

Synopsis:

Philippe, Thomas and Valerie formed a team to develop new concepts in the electric power delivery business. The project ran through the phases of study, design, implementation, and testing in the field. The project duration was six years, two years longer than originally planned. Over the course of the term, there were changes in the team members, though it generally remained at six people. Sometimes others were brought in for short periods to perform specialized tasks. Engineers Philippe and Thomas, and Valerie, a computer scientist, were the only people who stayed with the project from concept to finish. From the beginning Philippe was in charge of the hardware design and development, and Thomas was the expert in power systems. Valerie was in charge of software development. They all worked well together. Philippe and Thomas had advanced degrees in engineering, and Valerie in computer science. They believed strongly that the project would eventually bring success in the market place. The final objective was to create a new department within the company and start a new product line. They naturally felt they would have leading management roles.

Over the course of the project they struggled with financial woes, people changes and even technology changes. For these and sometimes political reasons, they changed organizations to which they reported. They started working for the manager of marketing and planning, then for general engineering and finally for research and development. The first boss, Manager of Marketing and Planning, was very supportive as he had much to gain by success of the project. The second boss, Manager of Engineering, was mostly consumed by the other work of his organization and didn't do much participating. He didn't interfere either, mostly just giving the team a home. The third manager, Harold, came on board after the system went into the field for testing. Harold was younger, egotistical and wanted to move up in the company. Harold held a Ph.D. in electrical engineering, had R&D (research and development) experience, but had no experience in power applications.

Harold periodically visited the remote testing site and always asked a lot of questions. He believed in visibility and always brought a camera. Once he even brought a professional photographer. Pictures and stories were very important to him. The team didn't take him very seriously, but thought of him as an administrative figurehead. However, they did appreciate his dedication to PR (public relations). They thought the PR would benefit them and the project. Over the course of the project, they had many pictures made of the equipment under test in the field. Harold still called for more pictures. He wanted what he called "action pictures". The team found out that what Harold wanted was pictures that included people. Once the team had a professional photographer make pictures while they appeared in different clothes in a series of photos as if made at different times. These photos sufficed for Harold to use for PR purposes.

Near the completion of the project, it came to the attention of Philippe, Thomas and Valerie, that Harold had had two articles published, one in a technical journal and the other was a cover story in a popular industry magazine. Pictures were included, but no other credit was given to the team. Momentarily, this didn't go over well with Philippe, Thomas and Valerie, but they were busy working on the project and didn't say anything. The three did share the patents granted for the project.

After project completion, a new business venture was started in a new location in a different state. This was the goal of the project from the beginning. A manager to head the new business was hired from another department of the company. The new manager shared credit in another article written by Harold. No team member was ever asked to participate, nor was ever cited in the article.

Harold received a fellowship award from a prestigious International electrical and electronics engineering society for what he claimed as his work on the project. The team members received no credit. To show their disapproval, none of the team members attended the awards dinner. They assumed that Harold got the message of their dissatisfaction. However, it didn't matter, as Harold got a company promotion to a higher level of management.

What Went Right:

- The team accomplished the technical objectives of the project under adverse conditions.
- The project accomplishments were transitioned into a business venture as originally planned.
- The project got PR.

What Went Wrong:

- The team got virtually no credit for the project, except patent awards.
- The boss took unearned credit.
- The boss' fellowship award shut out any such awards for the team members.
- The boss got a job promotion based on others' work.
- The team members were left where they had started, six years before, looking for another project to start.

Lessons Learned:

- Take time away from technical activity to do necessary PR (Public Relations).

- Don't expect automatic PR.
- Don't expect the boss to provide PR.
- Look into your boss's background and record.
- Watch closely what the boss is doing.
- Make sure that credit is received periodically, don't wait until the end.
- Develop a following of technical people interested in your project's progress by giving periodic reports.

Outcome:

The project was a business success. A new business was started in a new location. The last manager received credit, awards and a company promotion. Unfortunately no member of the team received any benefit. The team was left disillusioned.

Management Assessment:

The project team worked diligently on a project in which they believed, and under numerous hardships. They moved about from one management to another as economic times changed. All of the organizations to which they reported made sense. They finally ended up where they properly belonged with the R&D project.

The final boss, Harold, the R&D manager, perhaps did things that represented more closely the R&D environment for which he had been trained. He held the team together, helped the team bring in the necessary funding and provided PR for the project. Unfortunately he did not promote the team who was doing the work. He considered himself upwardly mobile and promoted himself by writing technical articles, and ultimately gained a fellowship in a prestigious International professional association. This, of course, caused animosity with the team.

Further, Harold could and should have used his position and influence to get the team involved in the transition of the project into the new business venture. The team got their personal satisfaction from finishing the project, but did not meet any of their objectives of starting and managing the new business venture.

After the project was over, the damage Harold had inflicted on Philippe, Thomas and Valerie had been done. There could be no easy recovery. They might have run a severe risk if they had tried to expose what Harold had done. The company and Harold had done what the Chairman and CEO had promised its employees, that is, "The company will provide a level playing field, and we're even every Friday".

In actuality, Harold was guilty of theft of intellectual property. He robbed the team of what was rightfully theirs, doing serious damage. In effect Harold had stolen identities and thereby crippled careers, a setback that can never be overcome.

What was the problem?

What would you do if you were in the position of Philippe, Thomas or Valerie?

- Nothing?
- Would you consider Harold to be dishonest?
- Would you go to higher management?
- Would you go to HR?
- Would you discuss with Harold?
- Would you expose Harold?
- Would you start writing your own accounts of the project?
- Do you agree with the Chairman and CEO?
- Other?

Case 16

ALPHA DOG:
The Micro Manager Boss

Key Players:

- Paul: **Boss**
- Gabe: Electrical Engineer
- Christopher: Electrical Engineer
- Russell: Electrical Engineer
- Courage: Alpha Dog

Synopsis:

Gabe, Russell, Christopher and Paul worked for the R&D (research and development) component of a large corporation. They had just obtained a contract to do R&D work for one of the company's businesses. The agreement was finalized at the customer's business facility.

The trip from the customer's plant back home was about a two-hour drive. This provided a closed forum for the engineers, Gabe, Christopher, Russell and their new boss, Paul, to discuss the events of the past two days, and plan for the future of the project. Gabe had finished a similar project a few months earlier, and was the unofficial team leader for proposing a new product development project for a new customer. Gabe knew some of the customer's engineers from past associations. It was through these associations that Gabe had been able to secure the new contract.

The engineers' previous program manager had been promoted within the R&D department. In order for him to move to the higher level, he was required to back fill his old position. He had chosen Paul who had a strong background in engineering, but this was to be his first management assignment. Gabe had found him to be a pleasant person, and he had sat quietly through the meetings with the customer engineers.

On the two-hour car trip back home Gabe started to brief Paul on the roles of the customer's engineers. He pointed out the political obstacles to expect on the project. He wanted to convey information that, if understood, would make the project run more smoothly. For example, there were two people who wanted to do the project in house, and did not want to farm it out to the separate R&D component. There was one whose previous work needed to be incorporated, mostly as a matter of goodwill. Gabe felt that background advice would be helpful and appreciated by his new boss.

Not so! Paul cut Gabe off abruptly, and said harshly, "That's past - I don't care what was done in the past!" Immediately, Gabe, Russell and Christopher sensed that the project was not going to go smoothly. Conversation was short the rest of the way home.

When the project got started, Paul didn't seem to contribute to the design, but rather slowed the process by asking questions of the designers. When one of the engineers would explain something technically, Paul had a habit of saying, "Well, I don't know if that's true or not." The team heard this expression over and over, and took it as an insult, as their integrity was in question.

One day Gabe forgot to attend a meeting that Paul had called. Later that day, Paul jumped on Gabe for missing the meeting. Gabe attempted to explain, "Oh no, I didn't have it on my calendar, and I forgot about it." To which Paul responded, "No you didn't!", contradicting Gabe. Gabe considered that Paul was calling him a liar, but he let it pass.

The engineers each had private offices. Most often it was convenient for one to run into another's office for questions or technical consultations. They liked to converge into one office and sketch a problem onto the writing board. On occasion, Paul would catch one, two or three engineers in one office. Most often it was in Gabe's office, as he was the oldest, most experienced, and had led the proposal team. They further believed that he should be the project manager rather than Paul. Invariably, Paul would fly into a tantrum and ask why a meeting was being held without him. They tried to explain that they were analyzing a small problem and it didn't require his participation. He would not accept it.

Gabe, Russell and Christopher, along with a fourth person from another group, had a lunchtime routine of picking up box lunches from the cafeteria and playing bridge in their conference room. Almost every day the game was interrupted, as Paul came in and asked questions about the project. He seemed to resent the time the team members took off for lunch and relaxed with a bridge game. One day a player at the table asked Paul if he could wait until the game was finished, and Paul exploded with, "Don't you tell me what to do!"

The project team would try to do their work while avoiding interactions and conflicts with Paul. They found some humor in making fun of their boss behind his back. For example, one engineer would say, "Good morning", to which the other would respond with, "I don't know if that's true or not. I'll have to look out the window." Or one would make the statement, "Have a nice weekend", whereas the reply would be, "Don't tell *me* what to do." They laughed at Paul's expense.

One day when Paul was away on vacation, the team of Gabe, Russell and Christopher went to see Paul's boss. They explained their difficulty with Paul and requested that something be done. They were working under too much stress, and the project was suffering. Paul's boss gave an explanation of why Paul was the way he was. Paul had been orphaned at a very early age and was raised by his grand parents and with no siblings. His grandparents gave him everything he wanted, and he did not have to share. He was home schooled during his early school years. He had no playmates with whom to get along until he went to middle school.

The team said they were sorry to hear about his younger years, but did not buy into the story. Especially when Christopher pointed out that he too had been adopted, and had no siblings. They didn't see any reason to be forgiving of their boss, for any reason, and certainly not for the way he was brought up from childhood.

What Went Right:

- The project team made the best of circumstances and developed the project.

What Went Wrong:

- The program manager, Paul, turned out to be a micro manager.
- The customer engineers learned there was discord within the project team.
- Higher management believed that Paul was doing a good job.
- Paul's boss listened, but did nothing.

Lessons Learned:

- It is extremely difficult to get rid of a bad manager.
- Actually making fun of the bad boss helped reduce the stress with humor.
- Anticipate the boss's moods and actions, and behave accordingly.
- Avoid confrontations. You cannot win under these circumstances.
- Keep the boss fully informed.

Outcome:

The project was a success. The resulting design and development was transitioned to the business department as planned. The business department made it into a marketing success.

Assessment of Management:

Paul appeared to be a micro manager of the worst type. He was an aggressive and driving individual. These traits were probably what got him the management job. He was totally insensitive to the feelings of those under his supervision. He did not know how to handle the role of manager. It is quite likely that he lacked confidence, and feared that in a management role, his technical expertise would slip away.

Before Paul's entry into the project as its manager, the team of engineers had already put together technical plans and had provided a winning proposal to a new customer. The previous manager made a poor choice in recommending his own replacement. When he was confronted with complaints about Paul as his replacement, he became defensive, and offered some excuses for Paul's actions. It would have looked bad on his record for him to have appointed a bad program manager such as Paul. HR was polite and took notes about the incidents, but did nothing, explaining that no laws or company procedures were violated, and it was up to the engineering management to solve such problems.

The project team made the best of a difficult situation. They had to maintain their professional conduct through the unprofessional conduct of their manager. They made light of Paul's behavior by talking and joking about his antics. The lunchtime bridge game was a good diversion from the constant stress, and it worked except when Paul came around. Eventually they gave up the lunchtime game.

The team did not buy into Paul's boss' explanation of a kid growing up without siblings. While it may have happened just that way, there is no management excuse for allowing Paul to continue as manager.

"Alpha Dog" is a designation given by animal enthusiasts to describe the animal that determines itself to be the leader of the pack, and is willing to exert force to be recognized as such. An Alpha Dog is usually trained to respect its human owners, but not other dogs. The term sometimes refers to people. The example below shows an analogy.

There was an aging Borzoi (Russian Wolfhound) dog named Gumbo (a.k.a. **Am/Can Ch. Mandolin-Moorland Stravinsky)**. Gumgo's owner's friend had a similarly aging female Borzoi, also AKC (American Kennel Club) Champion. The owners decided to get one more litter of puppies from the pair. They tried unsuccessfully at first, and then resorted to artificial insemination. The mating produced only one puppy, which had to be delivered by Cesarean section. The puppy, named Courage (a.k.a. Ch. Stardust Kurazh of Mandolin), was adorable and received lots of toys and human affection. He was special. But he had no siblings with which to play and learn how to soften his bites and rowdiness. Now, some years later, Courage, like his parents, is both American and Canadian Kennel Club Champion. He is well mannered and loves people, but he does not get along well with other dogs. He is aggressive and domineering and expects always to be Alpha Dog. Courage rules over any other dogs in his kennel, making their lives miserable.

Do people act the same way for the same reasons? Should such actions by people be tolerated?

What would you do if you were in Gabe's position?

- Nothing?
- Are Paul's actions forgivable?
- Should he be given some slack?
- Would you have a confrontation with Paul?
- Would you complain to higher management?
- Would you complain to HR?
- Would you look for another job?
- Do you accept the Alpha Dog theory?
- Other?

Case 17

POLITICALLY CORRECT:
But -- Deadly Gender Discrimination

Key Players:

- Willard: **Boss**
- LeRoy: **Willard's Boss**
- Pamela: Trainee/Assistant, Victim
- Bernie: Engineer, witness
- Alex: Engineer, witness
- Donna: Office Manager/Assistant
- Patent Attorney

Synopsis:

Pamela was the only woman doing technical work in the research and development laboratory with about fifteen male engineers. The engineers were considered individual contributors, many working alone on original research, or in small teams, which was common in the R&D environment. She had worked in the laboratory for about a year. At forty six years of age, she had a degree in math that was twenty four years old. She had early experience in her field of training before taking time away for about twenty years and raising a family. On reentering the work force she started taking courses in computer science and became a roving assistant to members of the laboratory. She was progressing toward becoming a computer programmer, and then a computer scientist. She did such jobs as entering code and data, and preparing Microsoft Power Point™ presentations for the engineers. She shared an office with Alex, a senior engineer. While she took her technical directions from the men, they all reported to the same program manager, Willard. She was well liked, got along well and did excellent work.

One winter day Pamela slipped and fell on ice in the company parking lot and came into the office with a skinned and bleeding forearm. She attempted to pass it off as nothing, but Donna, the office administrator, told her that since she got hurt on company property, company procedure required her to go to the dispensary. Bernie, an engineer whose car was parked near the front door, drove her to the dispensary. She received treatment and returned to work.

Some months later, in the springtime, Pamela's work started to suffer. She wasn't finishing her work assignments. She didn't seem to care. The men dealt with the problem by simply doing the work themselves. They could no longer depend on her to complete a job. She started showing other signs of inappropriate behavior. She came to work late, missed entire days, and sat at her desk eating veggies all day, letting the work pile up.

Then one morning she walked into Bernie's office, stood before him at attention, and sang a kindergarten song. Bernie thought that was an amusing joke, and laughed and clapped his hands when she finished. A few days later she did it again, and started doing it on a daily basis. He mentioned her behavior to Alex and discovered she was repeating the scenario with the other engineers.

Bernie and Alex commented about her odd behavior to the female office administrator, Donna. Donna had kept a dish of candy on her desk. They learned that Pamela had been eating all the candy (the entire dish full) from Donna's desk. Donna had to quit displaying the candy.

Alex and Bernie thought a medical problem was developing. Alex suggested that it was possibly a result of her fall on the ice. She may have hit her head. Together they went to their manager, Willard. Willard's reaction surprised both Alex and Bernie. Willard told Alex and Bernie that when he saw diplomas or licenses on their walls designating them to be medical doctors, he would listen to their opinions. Otherwise, "Leave her alone unless you're looking for trouble."

The problem got worse. Alex and Bernie took the problem to their boss's boss, LeRoy, who asked his office administrator, Donna, to talk to the HR (Human Resources) office. LeRoy either didn't take the problem seriously, or he simply passed what he considered a woman's problem to a woman for solution. The content of subsequent discussions between Donna and HR are not known, but it became clear that HR took no action.

Bernie happened to attend an out of town meeting and traveled by car with one of the company's patent attorneys. During the trip he brought up the subject of Pamela's behavior. The attorney knew nothing about the situation, but said he was not surprised. He explained that if the circumstances had involved a man, the problem would have been dealt with straight forward. A male manager would simply walk up and say, "I want you to go back for further medical examination related to your fall on the ice. Done. Case closed." He went on to say that since Pamela was a woman, everyone was afraid to mention the problem. All employees had been overly indoctrinated in what might be interpreted as a gender discrimination situation. The male managers were paranoid about even mentioning that a woman worker might have a medical problem, certainly not a mental problem, as a good way to be accused of gender harassment. That would open the door for a serious lawsuit.

Pamela's condition on the job continued to deteriorate. Finally, she stopped coming to work altogether. Her husband called the laboratory once and talked to Bernie. He knew that Bernie had taken Pamela to the dispensary on the day of her fall. He asked questions about the accident on the ice, and was told that no one saw the accident. He told Bernie that Pamela was hospitalized and diagnosed as having a fluid accumulation on the brain. He explained that it was not Alzheimer's, but she exhibited similar symptoms. Clearly the accident was suspected.

Within weeks Pamela was dead. Bernie and Alex blamed the company. LeRoy told Bernie and Alex to keep quiet about Pamela. They fully expected the company to be involved in a lawsuit as a result of what happened. However, there was no lawsuit.

What Went Right:

- The company hired a good employee.
- The company had good diversity and equal opportunity policies.

- The company provided training on implementation of policies.
- The company hired a woman employee in compliance with policies against discrimination in hiring.
- The company provided the immediate medical service as she requested.

What Went Wrong:

- An unfortunate accident occurred on company property.
- The company dispensary did not follow up on the accident.
- Two levels of management and HR did not use common sense.
- Management was unreliable in personnel matters.
- Management showed no compassion.
- The employee died.

Lessons Learned:

- Male managers are fearful about any decision relating to a woman's mental health.
- The company concentrated only on the legal ramifications of gender discrimination.
- The company should have a procedure covering such situations that applies equally to both genders.
- The dispensary should follow up on such accidents. A fall on ice may cause head injuries that are not immediately detectable.
- The current managers could not be relied upon because of perceived gender problems. This is a problem to be recognized.
- The male engineer witnesses should have protection in such situations.
- A lawsuit against the company more severe than gender discrimination could result.
- Workers compensation should have applied since the accident occurred on company property while entering the workplace.

- This is a case worthy of coverage in the anti discrimination handbook.
- Consequences of bad decisions can be deadly.

Outcome:

The employee died, possibly because of lack of timely medical attention.

Assessment of Management:

The company is obligated to provide a safe work place including parking facilities. There is no reason to believe that there was negligence on anybody's part as for the parking lot. It had been cleared of snow and ice by professional crews. Pamela had an unfortunate accident, slipping on the ice. She probably did not know she had hit her head, if in fact she did. Everyone followed correct procedure with the information known at the time of the accident. In fact, everyone thought that she had fully recovered, and continued her work as normal.

The real problem showed up when Pamela started to show symptoms with which no one knew how to deal. The laboratory was not typical in that it had about fifteen men and only one woman in technical jobs. Bernie and Alex were the first to recognize her abnormal behavior, and their first thoughts were of her well being. Accordingly, they took the approach that they thought would be effective in getting treatment for Pamela, or at least some medical attention. They were surprised when Willard made light of their concerns. It was in all seriousness, Willard had told Alex and Bernie that when he "saw diplomas on their walls designating them to be medical doctors, he would listen to their opinions". He avoided giving any reason for his position.

While Bernie and Alex suspected it, the patent attorney was the first to actually say that there was probable gender discrimination. Willard clearly was not willing to listen to anything Bernie or Alex had to say about Pamela. Bernie and Alex talked to Willard's boss, LeRoy. LeRoy said he would take care of it. LeRoy handed the problem off to his administrative assistant, a woman, Donna, as he intended to take the men out of the loop. The men would be safe from any claims of discrimination. LeRoy simply avoided the problem by turning the problem over to a woman. It is assumed that Donna called HR, but then she failed to follow up. LeRoy never brought the subject up. When Pamela quit coming to work, no one did anything -- except Alex. Alex called her at home one day because he cared about her welfare, talked to her and she seemed to be all right. That eased somewhat the concerns of Alex and Bernie. After all, Pamela had a husband at home, and if something was wrong, he should have taken care of it.

Alex and Bernie had alerted their management of the problem concerning Pamela, and they felt that doing anything further would have been in defiance. Clearly there was gender discrimination. It was not the type of discrimination covered in the handbook, but nevertheless it was discrimination of the worst sort. A woman's death may have been avoided. This was not the popular kind of discrimination where a person might be harassed on the job, or where a man might be favored over a woman for salary or promotion. The men in the leadership roles failed to do anything because they were afraid of accusations of gender discrimination. Maybe not under the law, but by doing nothing, they were in fact guilty of discrimination. The woman was not afforded the same kind of treatment that undeniably would have been applied to a man.

What would you do if you were in Bernie or Alex's position?

- Nothing?
- Did they do the right thing by going to their boss and then the boss's boss?
- Would you talk to Pamela about her unusual behavior?
- Would you contact Pamela's husband?
- Would you go to HR?
- What should Donna have done?
- Would you encourage Donna to do more?
- Would you talk to the company doctor or a nurse at the company dispensary?
- Other?

What you do if you were a woman
   reporting to the same managers,
   and observed what Bernie and Alex
   observed?

What would you do if you were in the
   position of either of the managers?

Case 18

SODOMIZER:
The Manager's Nickname

Key Players:

- Peter: **Boss**
- Steve: Engineer
- Bea: Computer Scientist
- Beverly: Computer Scientist

Synopsis:

Steve and Bea were electrical engineer and computer scientist respectively in a large company. Both had recently transferred from an all-engineering unit to a computer science unit within the same department. Their new manager was Peter who had a background in computer science, and was specialized in the field of artificial intelligence and, more narrowly in natural languages. He had some experience in developing learning machines. Peter had a Ph.D. in his field, but had no formal training in management, which was not unusual in the company. Steve didn't expect Peter to know much about engineering, but did not expect it to be a problem. Steve would simply work on his engineering projects and interface with the computer scientists as needed. Peter was expected to provide such management functions as overhead control, budgeting and making sure that Steve got paid. Peter had promised Steve a substantial salary increase when his normal salary action time came around, just as if he had stayed within his previous unit.

Steve began eating lunch with the computer scientists of the unit. There he met Beverly who was a computer scientist with expertise in Peter's field. Steve noticed immediately that much of the lunch table chatter was about their boss, Peter. Beverly quickly made it clear that she didn't like Peter. Others trained with Ph.D.'s and experienced in his field talked about Peter's incompetence, referred to him as "Sodomizer", and claimed that he was "brain dead". Steve noted that the derogatory term rhymed with Peter's last name, and assumed that they had made up the name because they just didn't like him. Knowing that computer scientists were an innovative bunch, he got a chuckle out of it. But, deep down he wondered if he had made a mistake by working for Peter.

The Christmas holidays had begun and Steve and his associate, Bea, found themselves working Christmas eve late into the evening in order to get a proposal out by year end. Peter encouraged them and offered a reward for their dedication. He told them to take their spouses to dinner at company expense, bring him the receipts and he would get them reimbursed by the company. That seemed to be a nice gesture, making them believe that Peter was an all right guy, as far as they were concerned.

Annual salary adjustment time came for Steve in mid January. Peter called Steve into his office and gave Steve a letter stating a salary increase. The increase was only one third of what had been promised when Steve transferred. Steve said, "I think you owe me an explanation." Peter replied, "I don't owe you anything." He then denied that he had promised anything before Steve's transfer. The meeting didn't go well.

Peter went on to say that Steve was fortunate, and that Beverly was not getting *any* salary increase. Peter confided that he had seen a fax to her in the outer office from a mid-western university. The fax talked about setting up courses and selecting textbooks. He had concluded from the fax that she intended to leave the company to join a university. Therefore, he would put money programmed for her to some other use. He could come in under his budget.

Some time later, Steve and Bea reminded each other that Peter had not followed through on reimbursing them for the dinner with their spouses as he had promised. Based on Steve's salary experience and what they both had learned from the lunch discussions with the computer scientists, they decided they had been exploited, but would not bring it up with Peter.

The lunches with the computer scientists continued with similar disclosures. On several occasions Peter was reported to misrepresent statements made by higher levels of management. He was known as a back stabber, a liar and not to be trusted with anything, especially personal information. Steve began to realize that while the nickname "Sodomizer" rhymed with Peter's last name, it had a much deeper meaning. It meant in business terms, that Peter was one to whom a person should not turn his back. There existed a great amount of distrust. A more polite term might have been "two faced".

Steve decided that his best course of action might be to get out of Peter's unit. He thought it would be easy. He started to look around within the department. He learned from two other managers that Peter had said bad things about him. Even though the other managers told him they didn't believe Peter, he still felt animosity toward Peter. Peter was indeed a back stabber.

What Went Right:

- The technical work ran fairly smoothly.

What Went Wrong:

- The manager, Peter, did not keep promises.
- Peter was a liar.
- He did not honor confidentiality.
- The manager was considered a back stabber.
- Bea was so dissatisfied that she found another job and left.

Lessons Learned:

- There usually is a good reason for a derogatory nickname. Check it out.
- Don't assume a manager with a different technical background will remain passive and not cause trouble.
- Don't use fax in a public area for private communications, use email or some other private means.
- Email may not be as confidential as one might think.
- A bad boss can devastate morale. It spreads around.

Outcome:

A confused state of affairs resulted. No harmony was in the unit. Eventually there was reorganization and Peter was ousted, though unfortunately not before Bea left the organization and transferred to another company component. Beverly left to work for a university leaving behind a letter detailing her dissatisfaction with Peter's management. Steve stayed, at least partly because Peter had run him down verbally to other managers behind his back, and he had experienced difficulty in transferring to another unit.

Assessment of Management:

The unit manager, Peter, had an unusually bad reputation among his subordinates, especially those within his own technical specialty. It is not known just how he appeared to the higher management, though they must have caught on because he was eventually moved to another job. He was not respected for either his technical or managerial skills. But, it was far worse than that.

He had been labeled with a nickname that was considered to be of the lowest form of insult that the subordinates could imagine. He was referred to as Sodomizer. Computer scientists are innovative people. The name went well as the word rhymed with his last name. That fact popularized its use – behind his back.

The term Sodomizer makes one think of the perpetrator of the act of sodomy. The word *sodomy* has acquired different meanings over time -- from Biblical to legal to business. Most definitions relate the word to sexual acts. However, this is not the context here. Many definitions relate the word to one's backside. In the business connotation here, it refers to someone who is disposed to acting behind one's back. In other words, in business context, the employees should cover their rears and keep him in sight. He simply could not be trusted. He did things inappropriately without their knowledge, ie., behind their backs.

Steve and Bea came into a difficult situation. They learned early about the manager's reputation, but not early enough to prevent their transfer into his employment. They soon experienced his actions, for which he got his name.

Steve and Bea made good faith decisions to join Peter's organization. They quickly realized they had made a mistake. The technical work for which they had control went well. However, the working environment under Peter was intolerable for Bea and Beverly, causing both to leave. Steve braved the storm and stayed.

What do you think was the problem?

What were the significant events?

Were the computer scientists justified in giving Peter the derogatory nickname?

Should Steve have told Beverly that Peter was reading her fax mail?

What would you do if you were in Steve's position?

- Nothing?
- Would you try to resolve issues with Peter?
- Would you tell Peter about the nickname?
- What would you tell the lunch crowd?
- Would you look for another job?
- Other?

Case 19

ATTENTION PLEASE: The ADD/ADHD Boss

Key Players:

- Frank: **Boss**
- Denny: Computer Scientist
- Wayne: Computer Scientist
- Harry: Computer Scientist from another group

Synopsis:

Denny was a computer scientist who reported to Frank, the manager of a research laboratory in a large company. Denny had a long history of developing software and systems to solve what are known as "hard" problems. He was experimenting with new concepts in high performance computing to meet future needs. Frank had recently come to the company from a job as an assistant professor at a prestigious university. Frank's employment record indicated that he had had five jobs since graduating with a Ph.D. in computer science. Denny had gotten to know Frank only casually.

Denny typically spent many hours sitting before his computer console running simulations of advanced concepts. His office was arranged such that when he was facing his computer, his back was turned toward the door, which was always open. Frank stopped by Denny's office.

Just as on numerous other occasions Frank would stop by and stand halfway in the doorway and ask Denny a question. Denny, in deep concentration, would be startled and then would stop his work to answer Frank's question. By the time that Denny had stopped what he was doing, shifted his thoughts to some new subject matter, Frank would say something like, "That's OK, don't worry about it," and would be gone as quickly as he had arrived. Invariably, this was annoying to Denny, but he started to get used to Frank's way.

Denny started to notice Frank exhibiting a behavior that he considered odd at meetings. Frank had a tendency to change subjects before all issues were resolved. It was as if there were an agenda that was timed with some undefined time allotted to each subject matter. Sometimes other people in the meeting were talking about a particular issue, and Frank would change the subject to something else. Very seldom was anything finished, and definite decisions made. There was never a summary at the end of a meeting. This also annoyed Denny, but he just assumed it was Frank's style of management.

Wayne was another computer scientist who reported to Frank. Wayne had been with the company for more than twenty five years and had experience in several of the company's departments. Wayne had a sense of humor that was appreciated and encouraged by the other people in Frank's research lab. The computer scientists liked to sit together at a big round table in the cafeteria and talk about the current events of the day. They enjoyed satire, and particularly liked to talk about the "dumb" things that the company and its managers did. Wayne liked to tell humorous company stories, sometimes drawing them out at length. Though seldom, sometimes Frank ate lunch with the computer scientists. On those occasions, of course, they refrained from talking about their current manager.

Over the course of the year, both Denny and Wayne had given numerous Microsoft Power Point ™ presentations to management and other company representatives to get their reactions and gain support for their plans. Frank would sit fidgeting and squirming in his seat, sometimes absent mindedly tapping a pencil on the table top. He seldom asked questions.

At a meeting with invited guests from outside the company, Frank laid his head down on the conference table and curled his hair with his fingers. He showed the outward appearance of boredom. The meeting was held to get customer reactions and inputs. Denny and Wayne were embarrassed by their boss' behavior, and later apologized to the guests. Fortunately the issues presented at these meetings somehow were resolved and the meetings ended with successful results.

Denny, Wayne, Frank and others were invited to watch a live demonstration of a new software system presented by Harry, a computer scientist in another laboratory. Harry sat in his chair at his computer with the guests huddled around watching the software play on the computer monitor as Harry narrated. Suddenly, Frank blurted out, "Hey, look, Harry's chair has only four legs!" This startled everyone, and then they all laughed. (The company had mandated that all office type swivel chairs have five legs for safety and insurance reasons.) After the laughter subsided, Harry recovered and went on with his demonstration.

Then came job performance appraisal time. Denny was appalled at the little amount of knowledge Frank had about Denny's work. After all, Denny had made many presentations of his work over the course of the year. Denny attempted to bring Frank up to date on some of his work, and tried to explain his plans for the future. Frank sat at the table and appeared bored. Frank finally said, "I don't like your presentations. They are too folksy." Denny found this to be strange, since he thought Frank, himself, gave the worst presentations he had ever seen, starting with "uh's and ah's" and then apologizing for his lack of knowledge. But, Frank was the boss. Denny left feeling that he had not received a fair job appraisal from Frank.

Denny told Wayne about his meeting with Frank. Within days Wayne came to the table for his meeting with Frank to discuss performance and plans. Frank started the meeting by saying, "Wayne, I don't like your 'stories'." Wayne was embarrassed, and thought, "what does this have to do with my work?" He shrugged his shoulders and said nothing. The meeting came to a quick end.

These appraisal meetings became the subject of discussions at the computer scientists' lunch table. The members of the group had all experienced similar problems with Frank. The telling of the incident about the four-legged chair had brought laughter. But they all knew that these humorous events were attributed to the one person who held their careers in his hands. The group concluded that Frank probably had an attention deficit disorder, known as ADD. That being the case, none knew what to do about it. One of the computer scientists had a discussion with a Human Resources manager. The HR manager listened politely, but did not do anything.

What Went Right:

- The computer scientists carried out their tasks.
- They even had fun.
- The computer scientists created the lunchtime forum for discussing company events, including Frank's behavior.
- Someone went to HR and complained about Frank's behavior.

What Went Wrong:

- The boss, Frank, exhibited behavior not conducive to innovative productivity.
- Frank was a distraction at meetings and presentations.
- Meetings seldom produced the participation and decisions sought at meetings.
- Frank didn't pay close attention to what his subordinates were doing and saying.
- Frank had an unusually short attention span.
- Frank did not implement a fair way to appraise the job performance of his employees.
- HR was of no help.

Lessons Learned:

- To recognize certain attention deficit disorders, known as ADD (Attention Deficit Disorder).
- It is a very serious matter if a boss tends to exhibit ADD or ADHD (Attention Deficit Hyperactivity Disorder) characteristics.
- The HR office should be made aware of ADD-like behavior.
- Major symptoms of ADD/ADHD are impulsiveness, inattention and hyperactivity, though not all symptoms need to be present.
- There are medical treatments and other types of therapy available.
- Company insurance covers mental as well as physical coverage.

■ It is estimated that about one in twenty adults suffer ADD/
ADHD to some extent. Only about 15 percent of those ever
receive treatment. This means that almost every workplace has
someone affected to some degree.

Outcome:

Eventually Frank left the company. His problem went with him to
become the problem of another employer. The computer scientists
continued with their jobs as the professionals that they were.

Assessment of Management:

The manager, Frank, exhibited symptoms of Attention Deficit Disorder
(ADD), sometimes referred to as Attention Deficit Hyperactivity Disorder
(ADHD). It is sometimes also called Adult ADD. The prevalence of
ADHD in adults is thought to be around 4.4%, according to the
Attention Deficit Disorder Association (ADDA). For more reading on
the subject, refer to:

Attention Deficit Disorder Association (ADDA), www.add.org.

According to the ADDA, the term applies to people who can focus
only on things that interest them, and disregard less interesting things.
They often experience problems such as a lack of social skills, an inability
to stay organized, or complete important tasks. These often result in
difficulty with personal relationships, even staying employed. People
may also stimulate themselves by doing reckless or dangerous activities
and thus complicate their lives with physical and legal problems. This
condition is detected sometimes in children in the early grades of school.
There are treatments readily available once the condition has been
detected.

Frank was ill suited to be a manager. All of his subordinates suffered
as a result of his actions, and lack of actions. However, he was probably
the biggest loser of all. He may have needed help that he did not get.
HR probably could have acted differently. Frank was assisted only in
finding another job. He would be better off if the new job were to be

significantly different from the manager's job. Most importantly, Frank should be able to recognize his problem and get medical assistance. It is also curious that Frank's family did not seem to do anything. Unfortunately there was probably nothing that Denny or any of the other employees could do except maintain an awareness of Frank's ways of behavior, and deal with it.

From medical and legal standpoints, the following applies. ADA (Americans with Disabilities Act) Law is mandated for employers with more than 15 full-time employees. Federal agencies are exempt. ADHD is recognized as a disability under federal legislation (the Rehabilitation Act of 1973; the Americans with Disabilities Act; and the Individuals with Disabilities Education Act).

References:
1) Attention Deficit Disorder Association (ADDA), www.add.org.
2) Department of Health and Human Services
3) National Institutes of Health

What do you think was the problem?

What were the significant signs?

Do you think that maybe Frank was just bored, or not interested in his job and needed to change jobs?

What would you do if you were in Denny's position?

What would you do if you were in Wayne's position?

- Nothing?
- Would you try to resolve issues directly with Frank?
- Would you go to HR?
- Would you go to higher management?
- Would you consult the company doctor?
- Would you look for another job?
- Other?

Case 20

WAKE UP:
The Power Napper

Key Players:

- Marty: **Boss**
- Francis: Computer Scientist
- Dick: Computer Scientist

Synopsis:

Francis was a computer science project leader who reported to Marty, the unit manager in a component in a big corporation. Francis and a small team of computer scientists were working on a significant project that, if successful, could be considered a major breakthrough in the field of parallel computing. The team was very enthusiastic about the expected results.

Reorganization within the company had resulted in Marty becoming the unit manager. Before the reorganization Francis and Marty had known each other, but only casually. Dick, another computer scientist had come into the unit with Marty, and had started working with Francis and his team. Marty was a very aggressive manager, and Francis's reaction was that he was fortunate to have Marty as his manager. Francis could tell that Marty put in many hours at work, as indicated by email time stamped late at night.

Francis walked into the manager's office and saw Marty was asleep in front of his computer. Francis tapped lightly on the door and said, "Sorry to disturb your nap, Marty, but I need your concurrence on something." Marty whirled around and said, "Sorry, I was getting my power nap. You know I put in a lot of long hours".

Francis was familiar with the term, "power nap". He had done it himself. It had become a term used by people who work long hours, and at various times during the day they would refresh themselves. Computer programmers have long sat in front of computer terminals and dozed off while a program is compiling, which sometimes might take hours. Actually, some compiler programs are left running overnight so the compilation will be done when the programmer comes to work in the morning. Francis knew also that Marty was under considerable job stress, with his new job.

Francis and his team of computer scientists reached a major milestone in their project, wrote a technical paper and announced the significant breakthrough for a problem that had been recognized for many years. Francis made a Microsoft Power Point™, presentation to computer scientists, engineers and managers. During his talk Francis noticed that Marty had dozed off sitting at the conference table. He paused momentarily and looked at Marty. Dick, who had known Marty longer than anyone else, spoke up. "Don't worry about him, he always does that." Francis continued his presentation, and Marty snapped out of his nap, as if nothing had happened.

It came annual job performance time and Francis sat facing Marty. He was astonished to find that Marty knew practically nothing about his major accomplishments. Marty accused Francis of not keeping him informed. Francis accused Marty of not paying attention during his management briefings. The meeting did not go well, and Francis left the meeting feeling that his work had not been appraised fairly. He actually was quite angry.

What Went Right:

- The project ran smoothly and produced results including the major project goals.
- Francis's team received external credit for their accomplishment through technical publications.
- Marty didn't interfere with anything Francis did.

What Went Wrong:

- Francis and his project team did not get fair credit from its management for the important accomplishments.
- Marty had a listening problem and did not understand Francis's project.
- Marty had a habit of taking his "power naps" at inappropriate times.
- Francis and the computer scientists considered Marty's behavior disrespectful.

Lessons Learned:

- Keep your manager informed of facts, progress, status, and problems – your job may depend on what the manager knows.
- Don't use presentations at big meetings as a forum to convey information to your boss.
- Use meetings only when feedback is needed from participants for decisions.
- Sometimes people go to sleep during presentations and lectures for a variety of reasons -- aside from sheer boredom, including loss of sleep, stress, or -- even medical conditions
- If the manager goes to sleep during a presentation, it may not be the speaker's fault, so wake him.
- Look for and recognize characteristics of *sleep apnea*, a medical condition.

Outcome:

The project accomplished its goal, but Francis and his team did not get the credit they deserved. Marty never learned what his problem was and did not take any corrective action. He eventually retired from the company.

Assessment of Management:

The manager, Marty, truly thought that he could work long hours and recover his energy by taking the short "power naps". Many people subscribe to that theory. What may not at all be apparent to the affected individual, may be quite obvious to others. That is, Marty likely was suffering from a medical condition called *sleep apnea*. Typically Marty would go to sleep unexpectedly while sitting straight up in his chair. Also he would awaken suddenly with a snort, as if his breathing had become obstructed. This is a symptom of something that could be very serious.

Sleep apnea is a problem causing loss of sleep, whereas the sufferer simply stops breathing, sometimes hundreds of time during the night. The brain has to wake up the body and tell the lungs to start breathing again. Before medical diagnosis, one with sleep apnea is rarely aware of having difficulty breathing, even after awakening. But the condition has a severe effect on the body. Symptoms may be present for years, even decades without identification. The sufferer may become conditioned to the daytime sleepiness and fatigue that results. He becomes accustomed to taking short sleep breaks at any time during the day, taking advantage of any inactivity. The proper diagnosis of sleep apnea is determined by a process called *polysomnography*. (See www.Wikipedia.com for a quick definition.) This generally involves sleeping overnight in a clinical environment with sensors strategically monitoring many of the body's functions.

The condition can be more easily detected at home rather than at work. Sleep is generally accompanied by loud snoring during the night. The air passageway becomes obstructed and then breathing stops. A brain mechanism interrupts the sleep to get the breathing restarted. Consequently, without the victim's knowledge, sleep is interrupted many times during the night leaving a feeling of fatigue and drowsiness during the day.

While taking short "power naps" during the work day, Marty may have recaptured some of his lost sleep, but was losing track of what was going on in the workplace.

It is far beyond the scope of this book to get into a medical discourse on the causes and effects of sleep apnea. A source of useful information can be found in:

The *American Academy of Sleep Medicine*, www.aasmnet.org.

Many famous entrepreneurs of the past have been recorded as going for long hours without sleep, by taking short naps. Currently much more is known about sleep disorders. Millions of people are now known to suffer from sleep apnea and other sleep disorders.

A treatment used in many cases of sleep apnea involves the use of a device called Continuous Positive Airway Pressure (CPAP, pronounced C-Pap). Nasal CPAP delivers air into the person's airway through a specially designed nasal mask or pillows. The mask does not breathe for you; the flow of air creates enough pressure when you inhale to keep your airway open. CPAP is considered the most effective non-surgical treatment for the alleviation of snoring and obstructive sleep apnea. CPAP is almost 100 percent effective. The pressure prevents breathing through the mouth. A variation on the CPAP is the BIPAP, which delivers two different pressures for comfort in going to sleep. CPAP's and BIPAP's are used by so many air travelers that airport security people are quite familiar with the devices. For more information start with the following:

The *American Academy of Otolaryngology—Head and Neck Surgery Foundation*, www.entnet.org

After discussing at length the problems concerning the boss, Francis and Dick were not completely without fault. Presentations of projects at meetings are not the right forums to keep the boss informed. Such meetings should be used for discussions among participants where decisions need to be made, or feedback is sought. Francis and Dick should have recognized the problem with the boss and dealt with it. They should have found time for individual discussions with the boss. Interactive one-on-one discussions might have been effective. To keep the boss appraised of their work, they could have initiated a periodic reporting procedure, such as weekly or monthly. It happens in many circumstances with professional individual contributors, that they go about their business with little regard for the boss.

What do you think was the problem?

What were the significant signs of a problem?

What would you do if you were in Francis's position?

What would you do if you were a project team member?

- Nothing?
- Would you look into what might be a cause of Marty's behavior?
- Would you discuss with Marty?
- If so, how would you go about it?
- Would you go to Marty's boss?
- Would you discuss with HR?
- Would you discuss with a company doctor?
- Would you look for another job?
- Other?

Case 21

RELIGION FIRST:
The Religious Boss

Key Players:

- Fritz: **Boss**
- Hildegard: Administrative Assistant

Synopsis:

Hildegard was a professional office manager. A long time employee, she was administrative assistant to the laboratory manager in a large company. She held a degree in business administration and had more than twenty years experience. She was good at her job. The laboratory manager had the opportunity for advancement in another part of the company, and he left the laboratory. A new manager, Fritz, a scientist with excellent qualifications, was hired from outside the company to take over the position.

From the very beginning it was clear that Fritz was not familiar with company procedures, nor was he expected to be in the short term. However, in that regard, he didn't seem to improve as time went by. This caused more headaches for Hildegard as his administrative assistant, though she performed quite proficiently. She tried to educate him in the company's operating procedures.

Over the course of four years, it was noticed that there had been a greater than normal employee turnover in the laboratory. Traditionally, entry-level people started work in the laboratories fresh out of universities with new earned Ph.D.'s in a field of science. Sometimes they would stay for a career, or they might take a project through R&D and then move out with it to one of the company's businesses. Others moved from

The Boss Is In

one laboratory to another as technical interests and funding sources changed.

It's not easily explained how one would know another's religion. One way, of course, is by meeting people in places of worship. It is strictly forbidden to consider religion in hiring, or even discuss such in interviews. Somehow it became common knowledge that Fritz was surrounding himself with people of his own religious faith. Certainly, Hildegard was aware. The individual engineers and scientists didn't care much as long as it didn't affect them. That is, until Hildegard was called in one day and Fritz told her to find another job. He intended to replace her with his buddy (of the same religious faith), who was available from a laboratory that was consolidating with another and didn't need two administrative assistants.

Hildegard was well known in the department, as well as her capabilities. However, because of cutbacks based on reduced funding, laboratories were restructuring. She was unable to find another suitable job. Fritz had assumed that he had all power over his position, and was heard screaming through the wall into the hallway, that Hildegard's job was to "find another job". Fritz's actions were not discussed openly until Hildegard's situation became known. Word spread rapidly. There were whispers of a "religious war" spreading throughout the department.

Hildegard scheduled an appointment with the department's director, who was a vice president in the company. She went to his office and there sat a company lawyer. She told the director that since he had brought a lawyer, she would come back later with her lawyer. She left his office and was informed later that a job had been created for her. Within a matter of months Fritz had been asked to leave. However, word spread that he was paid off and a university in a neighboring state was given a grant with the condition that they provide him a job for a year. The center's director was of the same religious belief, also, and it is thought that he considered Fritz's actions to be an embarrassment. His actions with Fritz caused the "problem" to be moved outside the company.

What Went Right:

- The company had good diversity and equal opportunity policies.

- Higher management intervened and provided Hildegard another job.
- The problem was recognized by the company's vice president in charge of the department.
- Fritz was eventually moved out of the company.

What Went Wrong:

- The equal opportunity policies appeared to have been ignored.
- The manager hired only his friends he met through his religious affiliations.
- The laboratory seemed to split into two groups based on religious preferences.
- There was stress on individuals to be "politically correct" at all times.
- HR (Human Resources) tended to ignore the fact that there was discord.
- Hildegard lost her job and had to settle for a different and lesser job.

Lessons Learned:

- Discrimination can be practiced in many ways.
- People don't know how to react in this kind of situation.
- Such deliberate action is difficult to prove.
- The organization may suffer in performance by reducing the size of the source of potential employees.

Outcome:

Hildegard was given a job created just for her. Fritz was paid off to leave the company. Reorganization caused the laboratory to be combined with other laboratories, eliminating the perceived problem.

Assessment of Management:

Everything that the manager did was so subtle that nothing of a religious nature was noticed for a long period of time. Then the subject started to come up when none of Fritz's closest associates were present. On occasion an engineer or scientist would make a "politically incorrect" statement about Fritz and his close associates, in a joking manner. However, in reality it was not a joke, but had become a concern that religious preference was being practiced. For those remaining from the time before Fritz was hired, Fritz was still considered a newcomer. No one had faced such a situation before and didn't know what to do about it.

Fritz could not explain the firing of Hildegard to anyone's satisfaction. Hildegard had some decisions to make also. She could have challenged the firing based on age, as she was over fifty and her replacement was not. She could have challenged the firing based on gender, as her replacement was a man. Religion was more unusual. HR didn't appear to provide any help for Hildegard, only explaining the options and benefits of layoff. HR did get her an appointment with the department director. HR may have done more behind the scenes, as there had been other complaints about Fritz.

The director did what he thought was in the best interest of the company. Perhaps it was also in his own best interest. He found, or caused the creation, of a new position for Hildegard. He then worked with HR and quietly eased Fritz out of the company in a way that was not embarrassing to either the company, himself or Fritz. It was likely to have been the least costly solution, also.

What would you do if you were in Hildegard's position?

What would you do if you reported to Fritz?

- Nothing?
- Would you go to higher management?
- Would you go to HR?
- Would you look for another job?
- Did Fritz's boss do the right thing?
- What should higher management do?
- Other?

What would you do if you reported to Fritz and were of the same religion as Fritz?

Case 22

UNLIKEABLE YOU:
The Boss Just Doesn't Like You

Key Players:

- Alice: **Boss**
- Phillip: Project Engineer
- Lindsay: Computer Scientist, AI expert

Synopsis:

Phillip, a project engineer, had finished a project and was seeking his next big and worthwhile project. He decided the timing was right to go back into a field he had left ten years earlier -- the automation of electric power distribution. Having power distribution and, more recently, Artificial Intelligence (AI) in his background, he planned to integrate the two into a project of "Smart Power". While AI was not his strongest suit, he attracted a younger computer scientist, Lindsay with an advanced degree in AI to join with him to develop the new project. Lindsay and Phillip reported to Alice, the manager of the AI unit, made up of a mix of engineers and computer scientists. They thought that Alice needed something substantial to put a big feather in her cap, and that she would be supportive.

However, it was a popular belief that Phillip and Alice did not like each other personally. Alice was overheard saying that Phillip did not like working for a woman. On another occasion, she was reported to have said that Phillip was like her ex-husband. Actually, Phillip didn't respect Alice's technical qualifications. Alice was not an engineer and had no training or experience in electric power, nor was she trained in management. With these factors in mind, Alice was noticeably defensive.

However, Phillip believed there would be very little interaction as far as the project was concerned, and Alice would be no more than an administrative manager.

The company had businesses in technical areas that would benefit from the project. They agreed to contribute funding accordingly. Phillip and Lindsay coordinated all of these individual businesses and defined their interfaces with each other to provide a plan for the "Smart Power System" development project.

Through his knowledge of the power industry and personal contacts, Phillip had significant advantages with both inside company and outside funding. The project was proposed and accepted, with incremental funding to follow. Phillip and Lindsay recruited several more team members with other backgrounds, such as communications experts and programmers to round out the team. Phillip believed that this new revolutionary project might prove to be one of the most exciting of his career.

As the project had just gotten underway, corporate headquarters initiated a cost reduction program. The cost reduction actually meant laying off people. Without much deliberation, Alice selected Phillip for layoff to meet a quota given by the higher management. Though Phillip had obtained a promise of project funding, the money had not yet come through.

The team, without Phillip to lead, later received and spent the initial money and then disbanded. It was an embarrassment to the department, and an outrage for the company components that had invested time and money. When word got around, other managers tried to take over the project, or at least take over the funding, but none was successful.

After leaving, Phillip felt that he had been mistreated and consulted with an attorney, who advised him that the company did, in fact, have the right to fire him -- just because his boss didn't like him. Nothing was in violation of the EEOC (Equal Employment Opportunity Commission) as far as the lawyer could see.

Phillip was laid off, and went into early retirement. A few years later a similar project was started with a new project team, but not under the auspices of Alice.

What Went Right:

- The several company businesses came together to enhance the businesses of all.
- The outside funding agency provided initial funding of the project, and planned to continue.

What Went Wrong:

- The boss, Alice, who was qualified only in a narrow field of artificial intelligence, didn't understand the electric power project.
- Alice had no experience with the outside funding agency and didn't know how such contracts were awarded.
- More than anything else, Alice didn't like Phillip personally.
- Phillip was fired.
- The project lost its leader, lost its funding, and it failed.

Lessons Learned:

- Projects need more than a personnel manager. They need a supporting manager who is knowledgeable of the project and how to acquire funding.
- Personal contacts make a big difference.
- It is always helpful to know the long range plans of the company.
- Sometimes it is better to fake a liking and respect for a boss.
- From a legal standpoint, in many states a personal dislike is justification for employee termination. The employee is "employed at the pleasure of the employer".
- It is probably better to never work for a boss who does not like you. The boss has all of the advantages. It is of little consolation that the manager gets fired after you are gone.

Outcome:

The project failed to continue. Phillip was laid off. Years later it was revived by new management and a new team.

Assessment of Management:

Most contract work is solicited from competitive bidders. One of the first questions a potential bidder might ask is if the procurement is "wired" to a particular supplier. In this case, Phillip had friends and contacts, who along with Phillip, put together a concept for a beneficial project. Alice did not understand the personal relationship that existed between Phillip and the funding sources, and expected that the project could run its course without Phillip.

In many states the courts side with the employer in that "the employee works at the pleasure of the employer", if no violations of the EEOC rules can be shown. Therefore, the company was well within its rights to terminate Phillip's employment. That is, assuming that there was no cause of Alice's dislike for Phillip that was prohibited by law, such as age, gender, race, religion, etc. Even though one or more of these factors may be argued, they may be difficult to prove.

Alice's action was unfortunate, not only for Phillip, but for many. There were the business components, the outside funding agency, utilities that would have benefited, Lindsay, and finally, Alice herself. Everyone concerned would have been better off if Alice had put her personal dislikes aside in favor of the many benefits of the project.

However, on the other hand, Alice was required to lay off somebody. She had to make a choice. There is not enough information about anyone else who she might have considered.

What do you think was the problem?

Should Alice have acted differently?

What would you do if you were in Phillip's position?

What would you do if you were in Lindsay's position?

What would you do if you were a project team member?

- Nothing?
- Would you try to resolve issues with Alice?
- Would you go to HR?
- Would you go to higher management?
- Would you try to resurrect relations with the outside funding source.
- Would you try to take over Phillip's job.
- Would you look for another job?
- Other?

Case 23

WHAT'S UP, DOC?
The Clueless Boss

Key Players:

- Wilson: **Boss**
- Michael: Project Team Leader
- Jack: U.S. Government Funding Representative

Synopsis:

Michael was a software engineer who reported to Wilson, a mid level manager in a big corporation. A U.S. Government agency for the past year had provided funding for new technology hardware and software in high performance computing for an important application. A leading U.S. producer of integrated circuit chips had developed and advanced the state-of-the-art hardware. Michael's software, coupled with this new hardware, showed great promise. Michael's project had received modest funding from the U.S. Government.

At the same time, the British Government was funding research for a competing British hi-tech company. The British company's advanced technology was in production earlier, but was not as technologically advanced. Michael's project had bought a British computer with their new technology to study for comparison. Michael's boss, Wilson, was aware of the British computer, as he had signed off for the purchase using his development budget. He saw it operating in the laboratory and had received Michael's reports on its use and evaluation.

A project meeting was scheduled with the Government funding agency in Washington, DC. Michael intended to participate and to request funding to continue the next phase of his software work.

Throughout the project Michael had worked closely with Jack, the Government representative, and the U.S. hardware maker.

Wilson was already scheduled be in Washington at the same time conducting other business, and therefore decided to represent Michael's project at the meeting. Wilson explained that that was necessary because of funding constraints. Michael fully expected the Government funding to continue for the next year, but at this point in time, funds were scarce.

There is no direct record of exactly what took place at the Washington meeting. It is known that Michael's boss, Wilson, became confused and mistakenly supported the British made product instead of that produced by the U.S. manufacturer using U.S. Government money. Needless to say, the Government's project manager, Jack, was displeased. Michael learned of this from a telephone discussion with Jack. Jack let Michael know he felt that the Government's funding was being misspent. Michael found himself in the awkward and embarrassing position of apologizing for his boss, Wilson's, actions. Michael was livid. His own boss was so clueless that he had sabotaged Michael's project.

As a direct result of the fiasco, the expected continuation of funding for the project was stopped. When Michael confronted Wilson, he denied that he had been the cause, though he sheepishly admitted his error at the meeting. Wilson asked Michael to not tell the other members of the software project team. However, they already knew, as Michael had already broken the news. The team had to terminate the project for lack of continued funding. Michael was left with the problem -- How does one reconcile with a manager who, through ignorance, destroys a project and Michael's job along with it?

What Went Right:

■ The project ran smoothly and produced results right up to termination.

What Went Wrong:

■ Wilson, the manager, was what is known as a "clueless" boss. (Michael's team had stronger words.)

- The manager did not understand the project, or the customer. Wilson did not have a personal relationship with the funding agency the way that Michael did.
- The manager made a mistake that was fatal to the project.
- The manager lied about what happened and tried to cover it up.
- One member of the project team was laid off for lack of funding.

Lessons Learned:

- Keep your manager informed of facts, progress, status, and problems – your job may depend on what your manager knows, does and says.
- The most qualified person should represent the project when funding is at stake.
- Get a meeting agenda, and prepare for such an important meeting.
- Be prepared if someone tries to shift blame onto you.

Outcome:

The project ran out of funds and died. Team members had to seek other projects. One employee was terminated in a lack of work situation because of reduced funding.

Assessment of Management:

The manager not only did not understand the project, but he did not know that he did not understand the project. For a meeting of such importance, an agenda should have been available in advance. Clearly, Wilson was not qualified to represent the work being done by his people. In light of the restricted funds for travel, it may have been more productive for Michael alone to have made the trip. However, this decision would have to be made by Wilson.

Wilson made several mistakes. He did not understand Michael's project, and made little or no effort to learn. He then lost whatever integrity he may have had by not admitting what had happened and not trying to make amends.

Michael was not completely in the clear. He should have prepared a presentation as if he were going to attend the meeting, and present to Wilson his request for continuation of funding. Obviously, there was no backup Plan-B to put into effect. Michael should have rehearsed the presentation with his manager. He should have been aware that his boss was clueless, and rectified the situation.

When a loss of expected funding occurs suddenly, it can be expected that there may be loss of jobs.

What/who do you think caused the problem?

What would you do if you were in Michael's position?

- Nothing?
- Would you try to resolve issues with Wilson?
- Would you go to Wilson's boss?
- Would you look for another job?
- Other?

About the Author

Robert M. Hardy

Robert M Hardy worked for major corporations for more than thirty years in a variety of positions in five different states in the U.S. His work ranged from NASA Apollo Space Program, high performance computing, electric power distribution automation, sonar and microcircuit chip development. Twenty nine years were with General Electric Company. He then counseled small business owners and managers for twelve years with SCORE (Service Corps of Retired Executives – resource partner with U.S. Small Business Administration). He has conducted Western business seminars in Russia, Ukraine and China. He holds BS degrees in Electrical Engineering and Industrial Management from MS State University, and MS degree in Management Science from FL Institute of Technology. He is a retired Professional Engineer. He was awarded the Honorary Doctorate by Uzhgorod (Ukraine) National University. He is the holder of five patents for his engineering in research and development. He is part owner of a joint venture (US-PRC) for business training in Shanghai, China. He resides in Winston-Salem, North Carolina, where he serves on the boards of several non-profit organizations, including International Sister Cities Program of Winston-Salem. He lives with his wife of fifty three years, Pat, and their dogs and cats. He shows his antique cars, and she shows her Borzoi dogs in various locations in the U.S. They enjoy frequent visits of one or more of their four grand children.